Th [illegible] Faith Bundle

TWO CHRISTIAN BOOKS FOR THE PRICE OF ONE

INCLUDES "JESUS ASCENDED. WHAT DOES THAT MEAN?" AND "BETHLEHEM, THE YEAR JESUS WAS BORN

SCOTT DOUGLAS

SD Publications
Anaheim, California
www.JesusAscended.co

Table of Contents

BOOK ONE: JESUS ASCENDED. WHAT DOES THAT MEAN?

Jesus Ascended. What Does That Mean?

JESUS' FINAL 40-DAY LESSON

ORGANIC FAITH SERIES
BOOK ONE

SCOTT DOUGLAS

Jesus Ascended. What Does That Mean?

For Miko Rey La Counte

INTRODUCTION

SOMETHING HAPPENED

Something happened.

Jesus rose. We hear about it every Easter. We sing songs about it. We even have an Easter Bunny to symbolize the event.[1]

But Christ didn't just rise from the dead. He ascended to Heaven.

We hear the stories about Peter and John and all the heroes of the New Testament, and they're unstoppable Christians—fearless and bold. And sometimes we wrongly assume that they just got that way. That Christ died for their sins, and bam! They're instantly changed! On the contrary, the disciples were actually quite cowardly in their actions after the Resurrection.

[1] Fun fact about Easter Bunnies—people used to believe that they were hermaphrodites (i.e., they could reproduce without having sex). You know who else could do that? The Virgin Mary! Hence, the Easter Bunny was born.

It wasn't until after the Ascension that they were on fire for Christ. So, what happened during the forty days? Something happened.

You'd think that everyone and their brother would want to talk about an event that incredible. But you'd be wrong. And it leaves us with more than a few questions.

Where do you go if you want to understand what happened? Matthew? You won't find it there. Mark? Kind of, but it's text that most Bible scholars now accept was not in the earliest version. What about John? Surely good old John would have a lot to say! Not exactly. He talks about Jesus doing miracles, but nowhere in John does he ascend to Heaven.

So how is it that Christians came to believe that Jesus not only rose from the dead, but stuck around forty days before ascending to Heaven? That's where Luke comes in. Luke is the only Gospel that talks at any length (even though it's short passages) about Jesus ascending. He does so in both the Gospel of Luke and the Acts of the Apostles, which he also authored.

Sprinkled throughout the Bible are references to the Ascension, which tells us that it was something early Christians believed. The Apostle Peter believed it,[2] as did the Apostle Paul,[3] and it's fair to say that all the other apostles did as well.[4]

---

[2] 1 Peter 3:13-22

[3] Ephesians 4:8-10

[4] See Appendix A for a more complete list of Ascension references.

So important is the doctrine, that the original statement of belief that most Christians (Catholic, Protestant, and Orthodox) go to—the Nicene Creed—includes it. That means if you belong to any of those groups, you are kind of supposed to believe in the Ascension.[5]

\# \# \#

A Not Completely Necessary Detour of Empty Tomb Theories

The point of this book isn't to prove that the Resurrection is real; there are plenty of books on that. Still, as a reference only, I will note the popular theories about what else could have happened.

The LCD Theory

This theory says what is depicted in the Bible is really just a series of hallucinations. That makes sense. It might even be logical. But there are two problems:

First, more than one person saw him—even 500 at one time. If Peter saw him but no one else did, it would be easy to dismiss it as a hallucination. But all the disciples (minus Judas) saw him, the women saw him, and strangers saw him.

---

[5] Even if you don't have the slightest idea about what it is or means.

Also, I've had some pretty weird dreams;[6] but here's the thing about my dreams—and the dreams of most people—they don't convict you to die for your dream. Hundreds of Christians had no problem dying for what they saw, and a vision just doesn't give you that kind of conviction.

The Thieving Disciples

One of the more popular beliefs amongst people who believe the tomb was empty, but that Jesus did not rise from the dead, is that his body was stolen—most likely by the disciples who were disappointed that Jesus did not rise on his own.

This theory makes pretty good sense. Your leader dies; you're in denial; and you don't want to believe you just spent years of your life with a false teacher...so you steal his body to make people believe it's true.

There are a number of problems with this theory. They were in a pretty hopeless place and didn't know what to make of the events that transpired. There is absolutely no reason to steal his body because they would gain nothing in doing so. Nobody would gain

---

[6] The one where my dog was my mother, and he (yes, for an even weirder reason my dog mother was a he) told me to become a doctor of medicine specializing in soda...that was a weird dream.

anything by stealing the body—not the disciples, not the Romans, not the women, and not the Jewish people. The gospel records Jesus' linens being in the tomb; why steal a body without the linens? "Hey guys, let's steal Jesus' body, but for good measure let's make him naked because everyone knows dead people like to feel the breeze."

The Swoon Theory

This theory says that Jesus didn't really die; he just fainted and was put in the tomb alive; after several hours, he woke up and left the tomb. The disciples only mistook him as being dead.

The problems with this theory are plentiful. First, the Gospel of John[7] says that the linen used to wrap him was still there—meaning that Jesus would have had to wiggle out of the wraps. And once he wiggled out, he—a man who had just spent the past several hours being beaten, hung on a cross, pierced at the side—would have had to move the stone away and further fight off the guard who was guarding the tomb.

So, what's the deal with the Ascension anyway? Shouldn't this be plastered all over the place? Wouldn't there have been

---

[7] John 20:5

a giant atomic bomb-sized glorious viewing that you could see all the way from Rome? Why did only believers see it?

First, it is referenced outside the Bible—more on that in later chapters.

Second, we have to consider the nature of Christ. He performed miracles, but that was never his ministry. He didn't come to Earth to be the flashy miracle guy. His ministry was the way he lived his life.

People frequently say, "If there is a God, then why doesn't he announce it?" What I often think about this phrase is "Doesn't he?" Every day, things happen that are beyond science—things that can only be described by the word miraculous. They deeply move us—heck sometimes we even like them on Facebook. But the thing is, miracles are forgotten pretty quickly. You are quicker to forget a miracle than you are a simple kind gesture in a time of need.

And let's not forget, if God did announce himself, the whole freewill thing would go out the window. If we could walk outside right now, look up and see God up in the sky, then why wouldn't we believe in him? But unfortunately, on Earth we can't have that kind of relationship.

So, in answer to that question about why people didn't see it from miles away, the reason is probably as simple as it was not all that spectacular. Jesus didn't ride up to Heaven on an atomic bomb with a cowboy hat, shooting out fireworks from his eyeballs. It was more likely a beautifully intimate moment witnessed by those closest to him. It wasn't meant for the entire Roman Empire to see.

# # #

So, we have this intimate event that only a select few even saw. Great. But why is that event even important?

Close your eyes and take a road trip through history with me; we're about to get Biblical, so buckle in.[8]

Think back to those early Sunday school stories; the ones about the fall of Eden, Noah, the Tower of Babel, Moses. They're great stories and even better lessons for history…but they also have a theme. The entire Old Testament has a theme, in fact. God's people mess up and they fall; God picks them up and they excel; God's people mess up and they fall; God picks them up and they excel. It's like a bad broken record. If you've ever read the Old Testament from cover to cover, you probably asked yourself at least fifty times, "Seriously, what's wrong with these people? Why can't they just listen to God?!"

The Jewish people were privileged in the sense that they knew no matter how badly they screwed up, God would eventually rescue them, and all would be well again. They expected it. The prophets predicting a Messiah who would rule over them should really not be all that surprising—of course God would send someone to rescue them. They had messed up, and the kingdom God had given them with David had been taken away, so of course a new king from David's line would come and rescue them. That's just the way God did things—God's redemption was just as predictable as Israel's sin.

---

[8] Don't worry, we'll stick to Sunday school stories.

The Ascension is the fulfillment of this promise. When Jesus left Earth, he created a new kingdom in the line of David in Heaven. This pattern of God's people sinning, and God's people being redeemed could finally be resolved once and for all.

Lots of men and women have been raised from the dead; the Resurrection of Christ is really nothing special. Sure, it's an amazing, unexplained feat that can only be attributed to divine intervention, but pause for a moment and ask: what's so special about the Resurrection? Christ raised dead people; so did his disciples. Yeah, it's pretty amazing that he rose from the dead, but if that in itself is enough to worship a person, shouldn't we also be praying to people like Lazarus?[9]

The amazing thing about the Resurrection is not the act, but the act that followed—the theology that feels more like a footnote in history: The Ascension. Which leaves us with a very important question to ask: If it's so important, then why is it only mentioned in the Gospel of Luke? Why isn't the Ascension mentioned more often in the Gospels?

First, let's consider dates. More than likely, Luke and John were the last Gospels written, which means they had more time to digest things. The Resurrection, by human standards, is more fascinating to tell, and there's a chance that the early writers of the Gospel hadn't quite considered the significance of what happened.

---

[9] Lazarus, for those who need a reminder, came back to life after being dead for four days after Jesus came and woke him up.

Let's also considered the missing fragment of Mark; it cuts off in a very unusual place. Most scholars agree that the ending in place was not by the original author…but most scholars also believe where it cuts off isn't the original ending. So, what are we left with? The most popular theory is that while the added text isn't completely Mark, it isn't completely not Mark either. What does that mean? It means there's a very strong chance that the original version of Mark did mention the Ascension—just not quite like the translator wrote it—perhaps with different syntax, but the same meaning.

The most important thing to remember about the Gospels is they were written with an audience in mind. Think about Abraham Lincoln; there have been over 15,000 books written about him. How can people still make money writing about Lincoln? Easy…they write about him from different angles that people haven't considered. Some biographers will spend little or no time writing about Lincoln's death because that's not what their book is about. So, when we think about why the Gospels each wrote different accounts of the post-Resurrection, it's because each one was writing for a different purpose.

# # #

The Audience of the Gospels

There's a lot to digest, so let's take a short break. As we consider why the Ascension isn't clearly recorded in all the Gospels, let's consider the purpose of each

Gospel (i.e. who they were writing to and what their intent was).

Matthew

<u>*Audience*</u>: Early tradition said the Gospel of Matthew was written by Matthew, the disciple; more recent scholars tend to believe that because Matthew seems to use Mark as a source, it may have been someone else.[10] Whatever the case, the Gospel of Matthew seems to have been written with Jews in mind; Matthew wanted to prove that Christ was the Messiah that the Jewish people had been waiting for.

<u>*Resurrection Message:*</u> The Gospel of Matthew ends with the Great Commission, in which Jesus instructs the disciples to go and make disciples of all nations. It's fitting that Matthew ended with Jesus telling the disciples to go and convert, because that's what his Gospel was all about—to tell the good news and teach about the new covenant.

Mark

[10] Such as a follower of Matthew.

Audience: Like Matthew, it's difficult to say who the author of Mark's Gospel is, but it's traditionally held that the author is John Mark—who was close to the Apostle Peter and likely based his Gospel on Peter's teaching. Mark's reference to Jewish customs that Jewish believers would already know suggests that Mark intended his book for Gentiles who weren't familiar with Jewish customs.

Resurrection Message: Mark's Resurrection message is the trickiest; not because it's hard to understand, but because it's hard to know what he actually wrote. The earliest versions of Mark stop midsentence with the trembling women who have found the empty tomb. Most scholars accept that there is truth to Mark 16:9-20, but there is debate about what was and wasn't in the actual Gospel. If you believe that the Gospel ended at verse 9, then the message clearly says that Christ rose, but there was probably confusion about what this meant.

Luke

Audience: Traditionally, the author of the Gospel of Luke was a physician and companion to the Apostle Paul named Luke. Luke was concerned with preserving an accurate historic record of what really happened. By the time the Gospel was written, there were a growing number of false teachings, and it seems that Luke set out to write out the real story for believers.

Resurrection Message: Luke paints a very vivid picture of both the Resurrection and Ascension; he obviously wanted the most non-biased, historically accurate report possible, so he also wanted to also give the most complete story.

John

Audience: The author's reference to himself seems to correctly imply that the Gospel of John was written by the Apostle John. John, by this point, had already seen the persecution of many of his Christian brothers and sisters, and it seems likely that he is writing the Gospel to build up those who believe while also earning new converts. John's style of philosophical writing is also appealing to Greek thinkers, so, while it may not have been his intent, it is easy to see that audience would have found the message appealing.

Resurrection Message: Like Luke, John also gives a detailed account of post-Resurrection events. John states the most important things but concludes on a hopeful note by noting that Jesus did many other things and there's absolutely no way any book could contain all of it.

While not all the Gospels end with the Ascension, there are plenty of references to it;[11] further the Ascension is referenced later in the letters and epistles. The intent of the Gospels was to tell the good news of the life and Resurrection of Christ; to the early church, the Ascension represented a sad time—a separation of the person they had devotedly followed. While writing a Gospel with the intention of converting a non-believer, the Ascension is not the most fitting in the story.

The Resurrection was great. I believe in it. I believe it was miraculous. But I don't believe that Christ is Lord because he rose from the dead.

There's more written about Christ's ministry before his death than the events that happened after his Resurrection, but when we look at Ascension, we begin to see that there's power in small details. We begin to see that something happened after the Resurrection—something happened to transform the lives of believers and make them more than followers.

---

[11] See the Appendix for a more comprehensive list.

The problem with the Resurrection of Christ is as believers we have a tendency to believe in the miracle and not the theology. When we look at what happened after the Resurrection, and further at the Ascension of Christ, we begin to see what happened to transform the followers—and in seeing this we might just be transformed ourselves.

Something did indeed happen during the forty days; why didn't God spend more time revealing? That's something that we will not know on Earth. But when we look at what he does reveal in the Ascension, we begin to see that Jesus was not done teaching; and as we begin to understand these teachings, we will be transformed ourselves.

UNSTOPPABLE CHRISTIANS

The apostles and first Christians weren't the only ones who were unstoppable; over the past 2000 some odd years, lots of Christians have done amazing and even miraculous things. In each chapter, I'll look at one unstoppable Christian you've probably never heard of.

It makes sense that the first person should literally be unstoppable. That brings us to...Denis.

Denis was the Bishop of the City of Love: Paris. He lived in the third century AD. Unfortunately for the Bishop, the City of Love wasn't so loving in the third century.

In 250 AD, the Emperor Decius issued an edict that said everyone must perform a sacrifice to the Roman gods. The edict is of note because it is the first time that legislation had forced Christians to decide between the church and state—or belief and death. The intended target was obviously Christians because Jews were exempt from such laws by having the status of religio licita (or permitted religion).

While there's nothing to support just how enforced the edict was, several very prominent Christians were martyred as a result. Because Denis was a well-known member of the church, it wasn't long before Rome came knocking.

Denis refused to perform the sacrifice, and he was ordered to be executed by beheading.

Here's where things get interesting—albeit divine—Denis' head is cut off…but he doesn't die! He picks up his head, continues preaching, and walks six miles before finally falling to his death.

A church was built to honor him: The Cathedral Basilica of Saint Denis in Saint-Denis, France.

ONE

JESUS APPEARS TO THE MARYS

More people believe in angels than in hell. And why not? It's far easier to believe in good things than bad. Unfortunately, most people believe in the Nicolas Cage kind of angels;[12] the kind of angel that humans can actually become if they're swell people; the kind that have wings and float around just waiting to save us. That's not necessarily false, but it's not exactly Biblical.[13]

So, when the gospels record angels at the empty tomb of Christ, it's important to remember what angels are in the Bible—to put it simply, angels are messengers from God.

There's an important lesson to be learned about the women Jesus is about to appear to, but before we get to that, we have to understand the angels.

Depending on the gospel account, there was between one to four angels at the tomb; contradictory, right? Not exactly.

---

[12] Fun fact—City of Angels steals several plot points from Hans Christian Andersen's *The Little Mermaid.*

[13] Meg Ryan isn't even a Bible name.

Remember, the Gospels are four different writers with four different purposes writing for four different audiences. They aren't contradicting each other; they're recording different aspects of the same story.

The greater importance isn't on the detail—how many angels there were—it's on the meaning of the details. What, if anything, do the angels mean? If angels are Heavenly messengers, then what is it that they are announcing?

First, it's obvious that their message is that Jesus has resurrected, and he is the Messiah. Just as gospels noted that angels were there to announce his birth, they are there to announce his resurrection.

But there's more. The Gospel of John gives an important detail in 20:11. He says that two angels were sitting.

Impressive, right? It's not every day you read about two angels sitting on the job. More curious, however, is not what they're doing, but where they're doing it—they're sitting where Jesus' body was only a short time ago.

It's time to get all Old Testament. The Old Testament is notorious for laws—lots and lots of laws.[14] Some laws that make sense[15] and some are a little…odd.[16] But tucked in there with all of those laws is a lot of stuff about a certain Ark of the Covenant. The Ark was built in Moses' time and they took that bad boy everywhere. It represented God's covenant with

---

[14] 613 laws to be exact.

[15] There's one God; worship him.

[16] They made sense thousands of years ago, but they really have no importance today.

the Israelites and it's a permanent fixture throughout the Old Testament.

So, what does that have to do with two angels sitting where Jesus was? On top of the Ark were statues of two cherubim—or angels.

What the Gospel of John is painting is a real-life Ark of the Covenant. They aren't just sitting back on the tomb's recliners—they're sitting on the stone that held Jesus' body; John's record is saying, "Guess what? There's a new covenant in town."

# # #

When Apple rolls out a new iPhone, what do they do? They hold a big press conference that's meant to get their base followers excited and then they'll go out and tell their friends who will also get excited, and before you know it millions of people have new phones. Every company uses the same strategy—market to your base—your product evangelist.

It makes sense that God would market his new covenant the same way—he'd tell his disciples all about it, so they could go spread the news to the world. But something unusual happens on the way to the podium to make the big announcement—God markets it to the audience you'd least likely suspect: the women.

It would be like Apple going to a third world where there's absolute zero cellular signal, Wi-Fi, or electricity and saying, "Isn't this cool?" I'm sure they'd think it was pretty amazing, but what are they supposed to do with it?

Today a woman is just as likely to start a revolution as a man; two thousand years ago? Not so much. So, what is God thinking? What's he trying to teach us here?

If you are a Bible conspiracy theorist, then it isn't at all surprising—Jesus was, after all, doing the old bait n' tackle with her; hints and blatant descriptions of Jesus and Mary locking lips are in all the ancient manuscripts. Unfortunately for Biblical conspiracy theorists, the ancient manuscripts come to light too long after Jesus' life to make them anything but just stories people were telling. The simple fact is there's nothing in the Gospels to suggest that Jesus was involved in a relationship with Mary.[17]

So, if it's not because he wanted to see his old sweetheart, then why? Was it because he was a card-carrying member of the local feminist movement of Jerusalem, and he wanted to set his boys straight on who he *really* loves? Not likely.[18]

So, what gives? There are 11 confused men who risk an awful lot to follow Jesus. Couldn't Jesus have done them a solid and let them know all was well? Of course! But he didn't…and that certainly begs the question why.

On the surface, the best reason is simply because the Marys were the least likely suspects for a crime. If one of the disciples had gotten to the tomb first, then people could have

---

[17] In the words of Seinfeld, "Not that there's anything wrong with that"—it just didn't happen.

[18] Jesus was pretty radical in thinking with regard to women, but his appearance here doesn't seem to imply it has anything to do with making a feminist statement.

more easily said they stole his body—heck, they didn't even go to the tomb first and people still say this!

The fact that it was a woman who was the first eyewitness makes it more believable for the mere fact that women would not be able to carry out the plot to steal his body—they'd have to roll away a large stone, carry a rather heavy body, and fight off Roman guards. There are plenty of women who could carry off this plot—they're called women warriors and they're champions in swordplay; Brienne of Tarth from *Game of Thrones*—she might be able to pull it off...but these women? Not so much.

But God rarely teaches us things on the surface. There's something much deeper and personal about what's about to happen. The disciples had a much different relationship with Jesus than the women did.

The first lesson Jesus gives post-Resurrection is about the relationship we can have with him.

# # #

Before getting too far along, let's address the elephant in the room. The women appear first in all four of the Gospels...kind of. When you read all the accounts side by side,[19] each gospel tells a slightly different story. Some mention that Jesus appeared in front of several women, others say it was only Mary Magdalene. Some say Mary went to the tomb, saw it was empty, told the others, then went back to the tomb.

So, are we really to believe that the Gospel is to be trusted when we have four different books saying four contradictory

[19] For added challenge, you can also read them all upside-down.

things? If they got this all messed up, they must have gotten the rest all messed up. That's certainly a fair point, but to call the accounts contradictory is a bit extreme—and wrong.

In reality, it can be assumed it was several women, but because Mary Magdalene was kind of like the Peter of women, that's who they mentioned.[20] As noted in the previous chapter, each author had a different audience; some of those audiences would have not known who all the Marys or other women were, but they definitely knew who Mary Magdalene was. It would be like a newspaper saying Pope Francis and Federico Lombardi flew to Germany to visit a church; Federico Lombardi is an important person in the Catholic Church, but most people don't know who he is—so what you are more likely to read is that Pope Francis flew to Germany to visit a church.

The different accounts are not an example of contradiction; rather, they are an example of different authors.

# # #

There's Something About Marys

Who were these women that all the Gospels mention? Let's pause for a section and get a pop-up mini biography.

MARY MAGDALENE

[20] She's kind of a rock star.

Luke 8:2 and Mark 16:9 say that she was a woman Jesus had cured and cast out seven demons from. Most see her as the person that women turned to as a leader in the early church—in the same way men might have looked at Peter. Some have called her a repentant prostitute, but this largely stems from the misunderstanding that she was the unnamed sinner who anoints Jesus' feet; most scholars agree that she was not. This misconception was helped along by Pope Gregory, who delivered a sermon that misattributed Mary with the unnamed sinner. Pope Gregory based this on the fact that the seven demons were really seven sins and those seven sins obviously represented her loose lifestyle. Speculation that she was in a relationship with Jesus was first seen in the Gospel of Philip;[21] in it, Jesus is seen kissing Mary in a way that offended the disciples who wanted to know why he loved her more than them.

SALOME

Salome is only briefly mentioned in the Bible, but the fact that she is mentioned at all shows that she is important. So, who was she? Depends on who you ask;

---

[21] Apocryphal text written most likely in the third century—so the first conspiracy theory about Jesus' love-life isn't documented for 300 years.

Catholic tradition holds that she is one of the Three Marys. The most popular tradition, however, is that she's the mother of James and John—she is also sometimes referred to as the sister of Mary...or Jesus' aunt. If you dig deeper into early Christian apocryphal text,[22] you find Salome mentioned quite a bit more; an infancy gospel called Protevangelion of James cites Salome as a midwife at the birth of Jesus. She is also often confused with Herod's daughter, also named Salome, whose erotic dance during Herod's birthday bash gave her mom the opportunity to ask for John the Baptist's head on a plate.

MARY, MOTHER OF JAMES

Mary is basically known for witnessing Jesus' death on the cross at a distance and seeing the empty tomb. Even apocryphal text seems to be mum on who she might have been. So, all we know is that she was the mother of James the Less.

JOANNA

Finally, it's worth noting that the women present for this event may not have been all Marys. Some speculate that one of the women was Joanna—a woman mentioned earlier in Luke. (Luke 8:2-3) Not a lot is

---

[22] Meaning that their truth cannot be verified.

known about Joanna except that she was married to Chuza, who managed Herod Antipas' household.

The angels just performed the opening act of the most epic rock concert ever—now it's time for the main act to perform his final set list of teachings before ascending to Heaven—and spoiler alert, his set list includes all of his greatest hits. In John 20:16, Jesus starts with a bang when he says something incredibly telling. He says, "Mary."

At first glance, it doesn't seem like much, but let's look at what's going on.

Mary is an emotional wreck. Her savior is gone. She can't make sense of what's happened. She's a mess!

Jesus appears to her and she's so emotional that she doesn't even know who she's talking to. She's in complete denial.

It's in this denial that it gets interesting.

Mary just devoted years of her life devoted to following this guy and now he's alive and in the flesh standing right in front of her…and she has no clue that it's him! That's a little odd, isn't it? When odd things happen in the Bible, we should never just shrug and say, "That was weird" and move on. We should look at it curiously and say is there something more going on here?

There's definitely more going on here. The scene is a mirror image of us.

When we don't believe, we're in denial. Jesus is standing right in front of us, but we just think we're talking to a stranger and we don't recognize him. We can't see Jesus until we are ready to accept Jesus. And in that moment, Mary just isn't ready because she still can't comprehend any of it.

But with one word, Mary snaps out of it. She can see Jesus and it all makes sense. She knows who he is.

Jesus doesn't do what some of us might. If I'd just risen from the dead and appeared in front of my wife and she didn't know me, I wouldn't say, "Diana." I'd shake her and say, "Are you kidding me! All these years together and you don't know who I am? What the heck is wrong with you?" And then I'd storm off and pout.

But Jesus says, "Mary." And with that word she knows Jesus is alive and standing in front of her.

Jesus could have said any word, but he chose her name. To snap her out of her denial, he told her he knew her name—he knew who she was. It's an intimate gesture and what it shows is that Jesus knows each of us personally. He knows our name.

But here's the funny thing about what happens next. Mary and Jesus just had a moment. It's intimate. It's personal. It's time to hug it up. But that doesn't happen.

The touchy-feely Jesus that's all over the New Testament is suddenly a little less…touchy.

There are a lot of polar opposites in the post-Resurrection—things you'd expect to be happening aren't happening.

Jesus Ascended. What Does That Mean?

Mary goes for the hug and Jesus hug blocks her. John 20:17 says that Jesus told her not to touch him because he had not ascended to Heaven.

So, let's get this straight. Jesus—the guy Christians grow up believing we can have a personal relationship with is telling her she can't hug him? That doesn't seem too personal.

At face value, it's not personal at all. Later, Thomas gets to touch Jesus, so why him and not Mary?

The fact that Thomas could touch him but not Mary tells us that when Jesus says not to touch him, it's not because he can't be touched.

Mary wants to embrace him because she thinks it's back to the good old days—chilling in the countryside listening to amazing sermons, feeding thousands, and getting tipsy on the best water-to-wine ever made. But Jesus is telling her that the good old days are gone—she needs to know him differently now. The good old days are really in front of her, but she needs to come to understand what that means.

From that point on, he needed Mary to know that the relationship would be a spiritual one—not a physical one.

There are two Jesuses. Some of us only get to know one. There's the one we all come to know—the one who did amazing things. One might call him the historical Jesus. And then there's one we know if we commit our life to him; this is the spiritual Jesus.

Jesus' refusal to Mary isn't because she can't touch him; it's because she can't touch him like before.

Everyone wants to see Jesus. If they could just have a bit of proof, they'd believe. But that Jesus isn't here anymore. The Jesus we can know is the one we know spiritually.

But the one we know spiritually we can know much more intimately than the one who came in the flesh. Before the Resurrection, Jesus was the great teacher; what's happening is the start of the transformation for believers—they are about to go from students to teachers.

And finally, we come to what may be the most jarring verse of all to some readers—especially modern readers who are not reading the original translation and may miss the context. Jesus gives specific instructions to Mary; he says to tell them, "I am ascending to my Father and your Father, to my God and your God." (NIV) [23]

Huh?

First, let's consider something very important here. Jesus could have just as easily said "our Father" and "our God." He didn't.

Let's hit the rewind button here a second and visit just a few chapters prior: John 5:16-18.

This is one of the first things that gets Jesus in a whirlwind of trouble with Jewish leaders. First, he heals on the Sabbath—a major no-no.[24] Jesus was a good talker; he probably could have gotten away with it by talking his way out, but he has no intention of running away. Instead he uses the phrase

---

[23] John 20:17

[24] Sabbaths are for obeying God, not experiencing God.

"My Father." That does it! The Jewish leaders are fuming because this phrase puts Jesus as an equal to God.

What Jesus is telling Mary is that he is equal to God…but he doesn't stop there. He is saying that the man upstairs is now "your Father" and "your God." Father is a reference to the divine nature of Christ, and God is a reference to his human nature (i.e., God in the Flesh). Christ has now secured our place and through him we can have unity with God.

Some of the Gospels simply reported that Mary and the others saw Jesus and he told them to go tell the disciples; that's essentially what John says. But John found it to be important to his message to relate what Jesus said to Mary.

John was traditionally the last Gospel written; perhaps in his old age, he had come to realize the importance women had played in Jesus' ministry and he wanted to portray them fairly. But more importantly, John wants his readers to know that they can have unity with God—that God doesn't have to be the mighty killjoy in the sky—that through Christ, we can have a relationship with God that's like belonging to a family.

There's going to be many lessons to transform the disciples lives post-Resurrection, but the first is about the relationship they now have with God.

Everyone knows the phrase, "You can have a personal relationship with God." But the nature of people can make that phrase carry less meaning, because Christians sometimes look at other Christians and expect them to have the same personal relationship that they have.

Having a personal relationship isn't about the other person. It's about you. Jesus Christ knows your name. He knows your struggles. Your pains. He knows your background. He knows what makes you angry; what makes you sad; what makes you want to give up—and what makes you want to keep going. He knows everything about you.

We all have struggles. Some of us it is addictions. Some of us it is pride. Some it is greed. Whatever it is: Jesus knows our name. He knows all of our weaknesses and he's returned to dwell inside us—to experience an intimacy with him that we would not know without the Resurrection.

But first we have to be like Mary: we have to see him. We can say we know Jesus just like Mary said she knew him. But knowing Jesus and seeing Jesus are two different things. We can go to church and know about Jesus—about his teachings, about what he did, and his theology; we can do all of that without ever really seeing Jesus—without ever really knowing what it means to have a true relationship with Jesus.

To see Jesus is to put all your pains aside and accept that Jesus really does want to dwell in you—he really does love you and he really is there with you. He really does know your name.

UNSTOPPABLE CHRISTIANS

Catherine of Siena is one of the top religious women of all time—right up there with Mary, Mary, and Other Mary. When most women of her day (she lived from 1347-1380) were content being submissive, she was quite the bad girl by actually using her mind and writing some of the greatest works of early Christian literature. Unfortunately, Catherine was also kind of anorexic for Jesus. Communion became one of her few meals in later life (and by later, we're talking late 20s).

Her fasting was legendary and ultimately fatal; by the age of 33, she could no longer eat or swallow water, and she died of a stroke. People of her day loved her—so much so that they wanted her body in Siena. But there was a problem—you couldn't just drag a smelly corpse out of Rome. Mourners decided that if they couldn't have the body, they could at least have the head. They chopped it off, stuffed it in a bag, and left for Siena; according to legends, when guards questioned what the foul-smelling bag was, they opened it up and there were roses inside. Fans of the morbid can see the head for themselves by visiting the Basilica di San Domenico.

TWO

CLEOPAS AND SOME OTHER GUY

We've heard the stories. Maybe we've even been the story. Something tragic happens—let's just say a bad accident. And in our moment of distress, a person is with us who comforts us and even helps us. Then they leave and we ask someone, "Hey, where's that person who was helping me?" And they say, "What person? You've been alone the whole time." In the words of the great philosopher Keanu Reeves: "Whoa!" What happens next could easily bring out the "Whoa!" in Keanu.

Jesus has just performed his opening act for the women—we can know Jesus personally, and it's now time for some time with his boys, the disciples. But about that...

Continuing on with the pattern of things not happening that you would expect to happen, Jesus doesn't visit his disciples. Instead, he appears to two somewhat random characters—one whose name is given (Cleopas), but who we still know pretty much nothing about, and one who's so irrelevant to the story, the name is not even mentioned.

With Mary, Jesus showed us how he knew us, but with these men, he's going to show us the place we need to be in to be able to see him. Anyone can "say" they have a personal relationship with Jesus Christ, but Jesus is going to show us with these men how we can prepare ourselves for an authentic relationship—one where we don't just know Christ, but experience him.

Luke 24:34 does mention there was a meeting with Peter before he met these two men; I'll come back to that in the next chapter. But Luke finds it important to mention this story before he references Peter, and he has good reason: the message here is important to both the spread of Christianity and our growth as Christians. Peter's meeting is personal; this meeting is transparent.

As with many things in the Bible, God doesn't reveal why he appears to these two random characters first. One can speculate that it's perhaps because the focus is on the teaching and not who is being taught—the disciples aren't the heroes of the Gospel, the message is. By not appearing to them it helps deemphasize their role in that message.

So, if the message and not the people is important, then what is the message being conveyed here?

Let's look first at where they are going: Emmaus.

If you want to go to a map, you can locate Emmaus right smack in the middle of somewhere. That's because no one actually knows where Emmaus is—or rather was. The city did exist; several sources cite various places with that name. The trouble is there are only theories about where it is.

So, is it so important that no one even knows where on Earth it is? That doesn't sound too important. And that's half right. It could have been Emmaus, or it could have been any other place. Luke doesn't tell us the name so we can all hightail it to the Middle East for a pilgrimage—he tells us the name so we know this is a true account. This event happened. He wants to make sure the reader knows this isn't a mythological story that is only symbolically or metaphorically true. If he had merely said, "Jesus met these two guys on the road," then one could interpret it as just a story. But he doesn't do that. These two guys had a destination.

Next, let's look at how Jesus appeared to them. Jesus appears several different ways post-Resurrection. In this appearance, it seems that Jesus doesn't just appear, but rather walks up behind them. Had he just appeared, then the story might have taken a different toll, because it would be much easier for these two men to see a miracle has appeared right in front of their eyes. Jesus doesn't want these men to witness a miracle—he wants them to have a connection.

It's the same connection we have. Jesus is God—do you really think that if he wanted to, he couldn't appear to you right as you read this passage and say, "What's up?!" He could! But he probably didn't. He doesn't want you to believe because of a miracle; he wants to really understand what the Resurrection is.

Cleopas and his companion take a lot of heat for not knowing who Jesus is; while these men aren't part of the core twelve, it's implied that they should have known better—they should have been able to recognize Jesus. But they don't. It's not all on them, however; the Bible says they were "kept" from recognizing him.[25] Why would they be "kept" from recognizing him? Let's mark that as "to be continued" and come back to it later.

Will the Real Cleopas Please Stand Up?

There are many traditions about who Cleopas was (and wasn't) over the years, three theories in particular have become popular:

Cleopas Was Cleophas — Hegesippus, an early chronicler of the church, wrote in 180 A.D. that he had interviewed a grandson of Jude the Apostle; the grandson claimed that Cleopas was Cleophas, who was the brother of Joseph (husband of the Virgin Mary).

Cleopas Was Clopas — John 19:25 references Clopas, who is traditionally viewed as either the husband of Mary Magdalene or the father of Mary Magdalene. She is recorded as "Mary of Clopas" which

[25] Luke 24:16

means, depending on who you ask, "Mary, wife of Clopas" or "Mary, daughter of Clopas."

Cleopas Was Cleopas — The figure so prominent in the story may have simply been an important figure in the early church who was never recorded anywhere else and thus his importance has been lost over the years.

Translations are a messy business and, with names especially, it's not uncommon for things to get lost in translation; all of these theories are certainly possible. It's also possible that Cleopas, Cleophas, and Clopas were the same person. Mary could have also been the infamous "Other Mary." Some have also interpreted Mary as the mother of Jesus and Clopas was her second husband.[26]

Cleopas and Mary — It's also possible that the companion was Mary, and Cleopas was her husband. Luke says they ask Jesus to "stay with us" which means that they seem to be living together; it's also possible that they are just related and sharing a home.

---

[26] Joseph having died.

Jesus uses many devices to teach—and what follows is indeed a teaching—the device he uses here starts by him quizzing the men. He wants the men to explain what they think had just happened.

If this is a quiz, the two men failed it. If you are a follower of Jesus Christ, and you just heard he rose from the dead and fulfilled everything he said he would, and you're walking on the road back home, then wouldn't you be talking about how amazing it is?! These two men basically tell Jesus all of that—but they miss the part about this being prophecy fulfilled. In reality, the two men are really confused. Like, seriously confused. Their great teacher has just been hung on a cross, and now there are reports about his body missing. It makes sense that they draw the logical conclusion and probably imagine that someone has taken his body.

Jesus—the kind and patient teacher—isn't so kind and patient here. He calls them fools. He's not subtle about it. He doesn't hold anything back. We often think of Jesus as a tolerable person, but he doesn't seem very tolerable here. There are a lot of reasons for this, but the one here seems to be because Jesus expects better of us. He's patient with the unbeliever, but when we confess with our lips that we believe in Jesus—when we follow him and trust in him—and then we act like these disciples and really let him down, he's not afraid to call us on our poor behaviors, or acts. He's going to call us fools. And even though Christ is forgiving, when he does this, it stings a little.

But he doesn't spend the next several hours lecturing them. He spends the time with them to make it right—to make them see as they should see. When our hearts are open, God will make it right—he will help us to see what he wants us to see.

Let's rewind for a minute. Jesus is back from the dead. He's suffered. And he's gone through what we can only imagine is some kind of terrible experience. If I came back from the dead, I'd probably start with, "Have I got something to tell you!" And then I'd proceed with this magical experience I just went through. So, you can only imagine what's about to follow this cringe-worthy scolding is going to be quite a lesson. And it is. But it's not what you might expect.

It's a Bible study.

Jesus often used parables to prove a point. He could be quite poetic in his teachings. But not now—when you'd expect him to be his most poetic, he's actually the most Jewish.

There is a place for parables, but right now the most important thing that needs to be taught is not what has transpired, rather what has been fulfilled. The prophecy of the Old Testament has come to pass.

Jesus turns to Moses—and all the prophets that follow. In Luke 24:27, it says, "And beginning with Moses and all the Prophets, he explained to them what was said in all the Scriptures concerning himself." (NIV) So we don't know what exactly was said, but we do know what this Bible study was about. We don't get to know what the two men were thinking—how they were reacting, because this story isn't about them.

Beginning with Moses, the Jewish people entered their most longstanding covenant with God. It's the one that introduced God's people to some of his greatest hits: The Ten Commandments, David and Goliath, Daniel and the Den of Lions—the covenant was a hit-making machine. But in between all these greatest hits were prophets who prophesied that something greater was coming: a new covenant. And with that new covenant: a Messiah. And this was the turning point that Bible study gave the men: *that Messiah had come*.

You would think at this point the eyes of the men would be open; but, again, that does not appear to be the case; they invite Jesus to fellowship with them inside their house, but they are not ready to say this man is their Lord.

So, in they walk into their home, and it's a classic, "Hey guys! Guess who's coming to dinner?!"

When you have a guest over for dinner, then you are—in a word—hospitable. That's not without reason. People have been doing this hospitable act for ages. They did it one hundred years ago; they did it two thousand years ago. So, what we should be seeing is these men and others in their home treating Jesus as a guest.

But in Luke 24:30, it tells us that as they ate, Jesus took the bread, "gave thanks, broke it and began to give it to them." That may not seem unusual, but this is not what a guest does. This is what a host should be doing.

Jesus is serving when he should be served. There's a lesson there that's often overlooked; everything Jesus does is to teach us what we should do. He's not afraid to serve when he's supposed to be served to—and neither should we.

Jesus has different ways of revealing his nature post-Resurrection—to Mary it was when he said her name that she finally opened her eyes and saw him. To these two men, it's the communion. There are lots of theories about this. One of the more popular ones is as Jesus broke the bread, the disciples looked down and saw his hands and the nail marks and immediately knew who it was. I don't think so. Remember, the Bible says they were "kept" from recognizing him.

Communion is one of the holiest sacraments you can take. Sometimes people take it for granted today. But if we're going to be Biblical about it, you don't take the sacrament until you've made things right with God.[27] You don't come before God while you still have an enemy you have not forgiven or a wrong you have not made right.

These disciples were "kept" from seeing Jesus standing right in front of them because they had to make things right; the communion symbolized them coming to the realization that Jesus wasn't just a great teacher—he was the son of God—the Messiah. Once they break bread, they are "kept" no more from being blinded.

But what happens next is key to this revelation. Jesus leaves. He doesn't say, "So now you get it—finally!" He doesn't proceed with more teaching. He leaves. Jesus knows how to make an exit! He leaves with the disciples' mouths hanging—with them thirsty for more. He leaves with the disciples on fire.

The disciples are burning up with the Spirit after this moment. They don't wait until the sun comes up to tell others what they heard—they take off to tell the others. And

---

[27] 1 Corinthians 11:28

remember, this is pre-Edison. There are no lights on the paths. And these are not the safest roads. But none of that matters.

What's the Deal with Communion?

Have you ever really thought about communion?

The history of communion can be both complicated and messy. Putting aside how often it should be celebrated, there's the question of wine or grape juice; the Bible says wine, but prohibition made that complicated—Welch's Food Inc., the multi-billion-dollar beverage company, was started with the sole intention of providing grape juice to churches. Many theologians (mostly Protestant) went to great lengths to explain how Jesus *really* meant grape juice when he said wine. The theological question of grape juice or wine is just for starters—others have argued whether we should use one cup or small individual cups; and don't get me started on the argument for what kind of bread should be used.

The question is, why is communion even important? The Bible certainly talks about it, but Jesus never gives the direct command: thou shalt break bread once a month—unless thy bread is discounted at the supermarket, and then break it before it's moldy.

One of the very few arguments for the frequency of communion is Acts 20:7: "On the first day of the week we came together to break bread. Paul spoke to the people and, because he intended to leave the next day, kept on talking until midnight." (NIV) This seems to tell us that Christians were doing this weekly, but other instances seem to argue that they were doing it even more regularly—whenever they were together.

The reality is, however, when we argue about the frequency—or about what drink should be used or if it should be in one cup or several—we're probably are missing the point of what communion is. Jesus tells his disciples to take communion to remember him. Are we going to remember him less if we don't eat a piece of bread dipped in wine or juice every week? Probably not. But when we think of it like that, then we're being selfish—communion isn't about us: it's about the community of believers. We come together to take it—to fellowship. Jesus broke bread and gave us perhaps one of the most telling theological lessons of what church should be: a place to come together and remember what Jesus Christ did for us.

The church I was raised in had a communion table in the center of the church—the pulpit was to the side of it; thinking back on this arrangement, it's clear what the point was: communion should be front and center. Communion is the church. And church isn't the place we go on Sunday. Church is the place we go to fellowship with other believers. Realistically, communion should be taken whenever we are with believers: at Bible studies, at church dinners, anywhere. It's the sacrament we should get most excited for. It shouldn't be a ritual—it should be a living sacrament that we celebrate and rejoice over.

# # #

Curiously, it's while they are *walking* that Jesus teaches them that they need to walk by faith and not by sight.

It's in the unexpected that we can see God's beauty. God is not revealing what man knows—he's showing us a glimpse of a reality that is beyond our understanding: a world where the unexpected in man's eyes starts to make sense.

Christ is around us, but we don't always see him. He's standing next to us in our joys and trials—next to us in all things. He's next to us now. But we don't recognize his presence until we need him. He knows when we need him.

And just like these men, he doesn't linger when he helps us. He gives us just enough to get us through, but he also makes us want more—hungry to feel his presence again—which isn't to say he leaves us: he's always there. It's in these men that Christ begins to show the drive that should be in all Christians—that would certainly be in his disciples; it's what will keep the disciples going when any other human who was not under the power of God would stop—and it's what keeps us going as well.

For these men, what stopped them from really experiencing Christ is not understanding the Resurrection. Once Jesus taught them about it, they were cleansed and they were ready to receive him. Jesus knows us personally, but before we accept that, he wants us to come to him ready to receive that—not to come to him while we're still holding grudges, or anger.

Jesus doesn't call us to receive him with a perfect heart—the fact that he knows us personally means that he understands we are coming to him with struggles and flaws—and he's going to get us through that. But our heart still needs to be clean. He has to be ready and open to receive what's going to come next.

UNSTOPPABLE CHRISTIANS

When it comes to fathers of the early church, you can't get any sexier than Augustine of Hippo. His timeless yawn-inducing works *The City of God* and *Confessions* have been required readings[28] for pretty much every seminary student since publication.

The mighty Hippo had his own encounter with God—though not on a path—and, in classic

[28] Or at the very least, required to purchase and put on bookshelf and said to have read and been greatly influenced by.

Augustine style, more bizarre than what the Emmaus Duo encountered.

Before you hear about the encounter, it's best to hear about Hippo's life prior. Prior to being one of the original kings of theology, Hippo was best known for being a horrible person. He was born to a pagan father and Christian mother. As a young adult, he became a follower and student of Manichaeism.[29]

Hippo got his Roman on at the age of 19 and began a relationship that resulted in the birth of his only son, Adeodatus; after years of being with his lover, Hippo realized it was time to man up and marry a 10-year-old. Don't get too grossed out by that—he was fully prepared to wait until she was 12[30] to take her as his wife.

A funny thing happened on his way to marrying his child-bride. Hippo, then 31, had been struggling because he felt his sexual desires had gotten in the way of his thinking; about this time, he met a bishop who showed him how surrendering to God could help him conquer all of this. It was a lot to take in, and he decided to chill for a spell under a tree; it was here

[29] A now forgotten religion that, at the time, was the main competition to Christianity; it taught the conflict of the spiritual world and the material world.

[30] Marrying age back then.

that he heard a child's voice singing, "Take it and read it; take it and read it." Nearby was Paul's Letter to the Romans—the verse he happened to see first: "Let us behave decently, as in the daytime, not in orgies and drunkenness, not in sexual immorality and debauchery, not in dissension and jealousy. Rather, clothe yourself with the Lord Jesus Christ." (Romans 13:13-14)

On the evening of Easter, Hippo was baptized, ditched his child-bride, became a celibate priest, and was one of the most unstoppable Christians who ever lived.

THREE

THIRD TIME'S A CHARM?

Third time's a charm. Finally, Jesus is going to get up close and personal with the people who knew him best.

But first, I must interrupt this regularly scheduled broadcast / chapter with breaking news: Peter. Because this appearance isn't *really* the first time he appeared to a disciple. As mentioned in Chapter 2, there is a vague reference to what has been aptly dubbed a "secret meeting" with Peter, which happened before Jesus met with Cleopas and his companion.

We know very little about the meeting. It's referenced only twice: "It is true! The Lord has risen and has appeared to Simon." (Luke 24:34) and "He appeared to Cephas,[31] and then the Twelve" (1 Corinthians 15:5).

So, if there's little known about it, we should just write it off, right? That would be careless, because even if we don't know all the details of the meeting, there's a lesson to be learned.

[31] Or Peter.

Here's what is obvious: Peter is the disciple who has been on fire for Jesus; he's the rock star of the group of twelve. But when the time comes for Peter to step it up and lead, Peter falls flat on his face and fails miserably. Not only did he just sort of back away and not support Jesus during his trial, but he outright disowned Jesus. But it's worse than that—he disowns him not once, not twice, but three times.

So, Peter is flying low.

When he hears Jesus is alive, there's obviously joy, but one can also imagine Peter feels as if he's been punched in the gut. He's heard good news, but then he probably realizes that his previous actions now have more substantial consequences then he ever imagined.

Still, Peter's passion is still there; when the Marys report the empty tombs, Peter sprints to the tomb to see it with his own eyes. It's worth noting that Peter likely wasn't fired up because he thought it was all true—that Jesus Christ had risen from the dead like he said he would. Luke 24:12 explains, "But they did not believe the women, because their words seemed to them like nonsense." The disciples, at this point, probably just thought that Jesus' body had been stolen or removed from the tomb.

So, Peter and John dash to the tomb. And this is where it gets a little vague. At some point after this, Jesus appears to Peter. What happened? Something.

Did Jesus speak to Peter? Did he just appear to him? Was it quick? John later gives the account of Jesus reinstating Peter, so one can easily speculate that this encounter was likely brief—something to make Peter know it's true, so he can slowly begin to come to terms and wrestle with it. But that's just speculation.

What we do know is this was a personal encounter. Unlike the first three appearances, where there are lessons for everyone to take in, this encounter is for Peter. The reader, in these instances, is not meant to learn anything other than the fact that it happened.

So, what's the lesson? What could we possibility get out of this vague and highly personal encounter? When we think about the reinstatement of Peter, we think of this immediate transformation. This character who changes at the snap of a finger. And that's sometimes how it can seem in our own life—people expect immediate change. But God didn't expect Peter to change overnight and he doesn't expect you to either.

God planted a seed in Peter here, and he let that seed grow in him for the next several days; so, when it's time for the forgiveness scene that most of us know to happen, he's ready for it. If there's something in our life that we need to change—or perhaps just an area that we need to grow in—God is already planting seeds. We're changing even if we haven't had this epiphany moment yet. And one day we'll be changed, and it may seem sudden, but God had been working in our hearts all along.

The Rule of Threes

Jesus rises from the dead in three days. Peter denounces Jesus three times. So far there's been three major lessons that Jesus has taught. There's a whole lot of threes going on. But we shouldn't read anything into that, right? The Bible is a multi-dimensional book. You've heard of 3D? 4D Perhaps? What about ∞D? That's the Bible. The dimensions are infinite and you should read into *everything*. It's the only book where you can have 12 people read a passage and get 12 completely different perspectives.

So, three? What gives? When three is used in the Bible, it's to signify completeness.

God is composed of—or completed—by three beings: The Father, The Son, and The Holy Spirit.

Before the flood—before the covenant God formed with Abraham—there were three Patriarchs: Abel, Enoch, and Noah.

And speaking of this covenant with Abraham? There's three more Patriarchs that come with that covenant: Abraham, Isaac, and Jacob.

It's hard to measure just how long Jesus' ministry lasted, but the Gospel of John references three Passovers over the course of Jesus' ministry; this has been used to say his ministry lasted three years. So, three again, could be used, to say that it took Jesus three years to complete his ministry.

The New Testament is God's new covenant with man. There are 27 books in the New Testament. That's 27 books to complete the book that completes God's new covenant. 27. So where's the three in that? 3^3.

The book of Revelations—that weird book and the one that ends the Bible, which has been widely interpreted and often widely misunderstood—it defines God as, "which is, and which was, and which is to come." (Revelation 1:4, NIV)

When you see three in the Bible, ask yourself this question: has something just been completed? Because often, the answer is yes and there's something to be learned from it.

# # #

And now, we return to our regularly scheduled chapter / broadcast—the moment we've all been waiting for—the most epic guess who's coming to dinner *ever*. Even more epic than the one he had with Cleopas and that other guy. Here we begin to see how Christ can really shape and change us when we are open to his power.

We've all been there—that awkward dinner where sitting across from us is the person we perhaps don't want to see, or perhaps the person we are just surprised to see. But what if that person is Jesus?[32] That would be pretty cool—certainly

[32] Quick! Hide the pork and make dinner kosher.

surprising. But let's add some perspective to this, because, unlike us, who know about the Resurrection, these disciples are still in shock and grief mode. They are confused. This guy they've been following for the past three years is suddenly gone—and more than that, he isn't what they thought he was: The Messiah. Because if he was the Messiah, then he wouldn't be gone—he would have become a mighty ruler.

The disciples are in a worrisome state. Unlike the disciples who will later go as far as to die in the name of Jesus Christ, these guys are gathered together afraid that any second the Jewish leaders will break down their door and arrest them. It doesn't say why they're afraid this will happen, but the most likely reason is the body of Christ is gone and the Jewish leaders think that they took it to start a revolution.

There was *so much* that these disciples needed to learn. Don't fret: they're going to learn it quickly.

So here they are. Alone. Afraid. Confused.

Jesus suddenly appears to them, and both Luke 24:36 and John 20:19 record Jesus as saying, "Peace be with you." (NIV)

This is the part where you expect the disciples to run to him! To hug him! To weep in joy! To worship him! But things, as you should be learning by now, don't happen as you'd expect. The disciples, instead of being elated, are outright terrified. In fact, they think he is a ghost.

This could have been Jesus' first teaching opportunity; he could have said, "A ghost?! Are you kidding me? I told you exactly what was going to happen and now that it's happened, you still don't believe? Seriously?! Come on guys!" But he's sensitive to their fear.

Perhaps you've heard a fire-and-brimstone preacher—a preacher who scares the Jesus into you by telling you if you don't believe, you'll eternally be burned and tortured more than you even know. And perhaps that works for some people. But what Jesus shows here is that fear doesn't work for most people; he's showing that God is sensitive to our fears and doubts. He's not going to try and scare us into believing. He's going to let belief come naturally.

So, Jesus is calm, and his first order of business is to prove that he is indeed *not* a ghost. He tells them to touch him and feel that he has flesh and bones.

Jesus is no ghost. He proves this here. But why is he no ghost? Why is it so important to show that he is flesh and bones? Even if Jesus could come back as a ghost after three days, and appear to people, then that would be pretty cool, right? God is spiritual. So why can't Jesus be spiritual? Why can't he just be a floating being that comes and gives peace to people? Surely you don't need flesh and bones to do that.

Could Jesus Christ have returned as a ghost? Would that *really* have been wrong? It's a fair question, but to answer it, first it's important to consider what the Bible actually says about ghosts.

First, ghosts are real. They're Biblical. In Samuel 28:1-19, Saul goes to a medium of Endor to call up the spirit of Samuel. The medium, or witch, is able to do it. But, it should be pointed out, she was able to do it because God allowed it—and things did not go so well for Saul because of his carelessness. There are other instances of ghosts in the Bible. Theologians have lots of theories about them; many would say they are evil spirits—not actually the deceased person. But what is clear is that God does not use ghosts to communicate with us.[33]

So, for Jesus to be a ghost, it would be contradicting everything God has taught believers to think about the spirit world—which is not to mess with it. Getting Old Testament for a minute, God revealed his message through himself; he didn't get some zombie kid from down the street to give it to them. To give this final teaching to the disciples, it needed to be from God Himself giving the message.

Jesus is God; but Jesus is also man. He has two natures. God manifested himself into the body of a man to fully prove that he understands man—to suffer as we suffer. In the Ascension, he takes this body to Heaven, but he's not gone yet.

Once Jesus shows them his hands, it clicks. They get it. Relieved, Jesus admits he's hungry. But is he really? Sure, he's just been in a dark tomb the past three days, but is hunger really what's going on here? It's important to note that "he ate it in their presence." (Luke 24:43, NIV) It doesn't say the disciples eat with him. This isn't a communion act, because they aren't joining in. Jesus is again demonstrating for them that he is the real deal—only a man will do that; visions don't do that; ghost don't do that; dreams don't do that. They've just

---

[33] Sorry, Bruce Willis fans…*The Sixth Sense* was *not* based on a true story.

touched him, but he needs them to know without a shadow of doubt that what they are seeing is Jesus Christ in the flesh.

The disciples had certainly heard the accounts by now of Jesus' appearance, but they were likely making excuses for them—the person was just seeing things and is in shock; but now they have proof—and missing fish to go along with that proof.

Now that the disciples have absolutely no reason to doubt, he gets down to business: it's time for a teaching.

Jesus isn't too hard on the disciples, but he does make it clear that this teaching shouldn't be anything new to them; in Luke 24:44, Jesus says, "This is what I told you while I was still with you." (NIV) Interpretation: "Come on guys! What part of *I'm the Messiah* did you not understand?!"

The disciples probably had their heads down at this point; they messed up. They should have known. John 20:21 says that Jesus said again "Peace be with you!" He knew what they were thinking, and he's telling them now that it's okay—they are forgiven: God is with them.

The Book of Acts tell us that the Holy Spirit descended on the Apostles at Pentecost. That's true. But it could really be argued that Pentecost begins on this night. Both Luke and John tell us that Jesus opened the minds of the disciples, but John 20:22 goes deeper and says he told them to "Receive the Holy Spirit." (NIV)

This passage is the most telling teaching that has happened so far. In every instance that Jesus reveals himself, minds are being opened, but it is with John that we see what happens when minds are opened.

Consider for a moment, the passage: Receive the Holy Spirit.

What does that mean to you?

It's unfortunate that in the mad dash of the world that we often are so focused on getting people to believe in God that we don't consider that a person must also receive God. Just because you go to some Bible crusade and go to the front of the church to say you believe in Jesus Christ doesn't mean that you are saved.

A person can believe in Jesus Christ—they can believe in God—they can even obey the commandments—and not be saved. That may seem a little unorthodox, but it's only because we are often taught a very watered-down version of the Bible. But all of this is very Biblical.

In Acts 8, the author tells the story of a sorcerer named Simon, who became a believer after he heard about Christ from Phillip. But that word "believer" is important here, because the passage goes on to say in Acts 8:14-17:

> When the apostles in Jerusalem heard that Samaria had accepted the word of God, they sent Peter and John to Samaria. When they arrived, they prayed for the new believers there that they might receive the Holy Spirit, because the Holy Spirit had not yet come to any of them; they had simply been baptized in the name of the Lord Jesus.

Salvation is really a two-step process; sometimes these steps happen together, and sometimes it takes time for the second to happen. Perhaps the best verse on what salvation is is Romans 10:9 which says that "If you declare with your mouth, 'Jesus is Lord,' and believe in your heart that God raised him from the dead, you will be saved." The verse shows the two steps to salvation:

Step One: Believe outwardly.

Step Two: Receive inwardly.

This process isn't unique to you and me—this is something that applies to even the disciples and early believers. For the past three some odd years, these disciples had been following Jesus. They believed in him.

In Luke 24:44, Jesus teaches them, "Everything must be fulfilled that is written about me in the Law of Moses, the Prophets and the Psalms." (NIV) And again, they believe. But they haven't received.

When Jesus stood in front of them—when he revealed himself to Mary(s), the man and the companion, and finally to the disciples—they each had their eyes opened. And they believed. But they had not received.

With the disciples, the reader is seeing for the first time more concretely what the next forty days will be about: receiving the Holy Spirit.

Many times, people accept Christ, and they're on fire—they're ready to go out and preach the good news! They're willing to die for the cross. These are exactly the type of people God wants, right? Not so fast. Because Christ doesn't say, "Okay boys! Have at 'em!" Luke 24:49 clarifies that while they will receive the Holy Spirit (i.e. what the Father has promised in verse 49), they are to "stay in the city until you have been clothed with the power from on high." What does that mean? It means they're fired up, but that doesn't mean that they are ready.

Jesus Ascended. What Does That Mean?

When we receive the Holy Spirit, we must pause and consider it. Pray. Mediate. Be still. Be silent. God wants us to spread the Word; he wants us to go out into the world. But he also wants us to be close to him. The disciples were no doubt fired up, but first they needed to connect with God. They had a relationship with God on Earth, and now they would need to understand what it means to have a relationship with God in Heaven.

There would come a time to go out into the world. Jesus tells them they will go out to the world and "If you forgive anyone's sins, their sins are forgiven; if you do not forgive them, they are not forgiven." (John 20:23)

That passage is easy to misinterpret. In fact, it can be used as ammo to condemn a person who you think is not acting in a manner that is…like you. This verse isn't about believers getting to have the rule of condemnation—about telling people who suffer from any kind of sin that they are going to burn in hell.

To be clear: only God has the ability to forgive. Man has only the ability to preach God's forgiveness.

So, what's going on here? Jesus is not telling them that they get to be judges. And he's not addressing each person personally. What's lost in translation is there is a plural word being used; in other words, he is saying as a community of believers (i.e., the church). What does the church have the ability to do? Tell people that God loves them, and that God forgives them.

He's telling them that through the Spirit, they can go out to the world and tell people that if they believe in the message and receive the Spirit, then they are forgiven—because this is what God has already said. He's not giving them the ability to invent or interpret what is right and wrong. Right and wrong here is unique to only one thing: believing in the Message.

When it says that if "they don't forgive, then they are not forgiven," it's not saying, "aren't you powerful! You have the ability to decide." It's saying if you tell someone about the Message of Christ and they reject it, then they are not forgiven.

# # #

Christ has now had three documented encounters,[34] and the order of when and why they happened seems clearer. First, Jesus appeared to individuals; it was personal. Second, Jesus appeared to a small company. And third, Jesus appeared to an assembled community. The order is showing how the Gospel is effectively spread: first, believers talk with a person at an individual, intimate level; then at a slightly larger level—with one or two others who can help us work through our doubts; and finally, in the fellowship of a larger gathering where it all comes together.

In the first encounter, Jesus is the friend. Just as when we first believed, it was probably because a friend came to us and told us at the most personal level what we believed. In the next encounter, Jesus is a teacher; and this, too, is really the next level most of us take—we heard it from a friend and it

---

[34] Not counting Peter, which is referenced, but for which the details are not documented.

sounds pretty solid, but we want to go and hear more. Finally, in the last encounter, Jesus is the Master; we believe and now it's time for us to go beyond belief and receive him, and be called to be sent out to proclaim the good news for the world.

UNSTOPPABLE CHRISTIANS

Preachers today don't have it so bad. At megachurches, they have speakers in places larger than some Cineplex's; they have jumbo screens to emphasize their points; some even have teleprompters with pages of notes.

Preachers today are no match for one of the greatest preachers who ever lived: Charles Spurgeon.

Spurgeon's sermons were just as legendary as the way he executed them. Think of the largest church you've been to. Then think bigger. Then think, this guy's preaching with no mic. Once you're there, then you can start to have an idea for the way Spurgeon preached.

By the age of 22, Spurgeon had grown a dwindling church to a church with thousands of regular congregants; he also had published a collection of sermons. His sermons were so popular, they were published and distributed in print weekly.

Spurgeon, at the cost of losing followers and having a decline in the sale of his sermons, vocally opposed slavery.

It was not uncommon for more than 10,000 people to show up and hear him preach. At his largest gathering (at London's Crystal Palace), 23,654 were recorded showing up—and he preached to them with no microphone.[35]

While Spurgeon did typically prepare his sermons in advance, he only went to the pulpit with one notecard that had an outline; with this short outline, he would preach for about forty minutes.

Spurgeon's sons, while never reaching the popularity of their father, also became pastors.

[35] Microphones weren't widely available until after his death.

FOUR

DOUBTS AND ALL

Nothing exciting ever happened at my college. So, when I heard a real-time Hollywood movie was being shot on campus, I was more than a little excited. David Duchovny was there! And Ivan Reitman was directing it.[36]

But I found out too late.

By the time I got to the shooting location, it was all packed up and only the guys packing everything up were there.

I missed out.

My missing out was a big deal at the time—albeit a nerdy missing out—but nothing compared to Thomas. Thomas had history's most epic "missed out." He missed out on seeing Jesus.

The Bible doesn't say why. I imagine how much more crushing it would be when we discover where Thomas was. How would you feel if you stayed home from church because it was the season finale of *Game of Thrones* and this was the night that Jesus showed up to give a sermon? I'm pretty sure

---

[36] It was called *Evolution.*

Thomas wasn't watching *Game of Thrones*, but perhaps it was worse—perhaps he missed out because he was too cowardly to be associated with the disciples. Perhaps he was in hiding.

We don't know the whole story; still, there's a lesson not only in Thomas' doubt, but what prevented Thomas from being with the other disciples. I think Thomas was in a place where we've all been: a place of comfort. Jesus was a great teacher, and it was great while it lasted, but now he's gone, and Thomas is going to get out while he still could.

When the disciples come to him and say that Jesus is alive, he doubts entirely. But is it doubt alone that is causing his resistance? Or is it the fact that if it's true, then he'll have to maybe do something about it?

We've all had those moments when we're driving down the highway and we see a homeless person begging for money. And we've all had the thought: they're probably not even homeless—they probably will just spend the money on booze and drugs. I've had the thought more times than I'd care to admit. Realistically, I don't want to know where the money will go. I don't want to know their story—that it will actually go to feed their child, or give them shelter, or simply just feed them; I want to know that it will go to booze and drugs. I want to know this because it's far easier to just believe they are bad people or that they deserve to be where they are.

When faced with reality it's far easier to make excuses than to face truth. It's far easier to just deny. If I went to an atheist and said, "God is real!" for many it's far easier to just deny it and not ask me why I believe this. If they deny it, then they can just go on believing it's not true; but if they ask me why, there's a chance I might be able to prove it—and that could knock them out of their comfort zone.

So, when Thomas hears from the other disciples that they have seen Jesus alive and well, he takes the easy—comfortable—path. He says, "Unless I see the nail marks in his hands and put my finger where the nails were, and put my hand into his side, I will not believe." (John 20:25, NIV) The fact that Thomas wants to put his hands where the nail marks were, seems to imply that Thomas didn't doubt that they saw "something" but he probably just thought they were a little delusional—it had, after all, been an emotional few days.

Time goes by. I imagine Thomas has gotten pretty pouty. The disciples are probably going on and on about how miraculous it is that Jesus appeared. And he's the odd man out. He's still doubting, for sure, but he's also feeling alone. These guys he's had a great bond with for the past several years are changing, and he's just the same old Thomas.

As the disciples are going joyfully around, there's probably something else that Thomas is feeling: empty. He picked feeling comfortable. He picked making an excuse. And that didn't get him anything but bitterness and loneliness.

# # #

My wife and I started going to a new church a few years back. It was big—the kind with plush seats and cushy backs. It was nice. But it was all too easy to get comfortable; to just recline in the seat, listen to the message, and go home. It didn't take long for us to look at each other and say, "I don't really feel anything here."

It wasn't the church's fault. It was our fault. A Sunday message isn't going to change you. It's not even going to transform you. Think about the Sermon on the Mount; think about any of Jesus' sermons. Sorry to interrupt you here, Kanye, but Jesus is the greatest preacher of *all* time! But it wasn't the sermons that transformed his disciples. It was when they combined those sermons with their actions. When my wife and I started volunteering, then our hearts changed and the church wasn't quite so comfortable. It was what we needed.

So, Thomas is sitting here, and he's comfortably empty. He has heard the greatest sermons from the greatest preacher, but that's not enough. Because if you hear the sermons but don't act on them, it's meaningless.

Then out of nowhere Jesus comes and after telling them "Peace be with you!" he doesn't waste any time. He goes straight to Thomas and says, "Put your finger here; see my hands. Reach out your hand and put it into my side. Stop doubting and believe." (John 20:26-27, NIV)

You have to wonder if Thomas wanted a take-back at this point. I know I would have. If Jesus stood in front of me, and said, "Go ahead—stick your fingers in the nail holes," I would probably take a few steps back and say, "I'm good, Lord—I was just kidding about that whole finger through the nail marks thing—that's a little too morbid for me!"

John doesn't record what happened—if Thomas actually touched him. But that's not important. He could have just stared dumbfounded for several minutes. What's important is what Thomas said, "My Lord and my God!" (John 20:28)—Thomas believed.

This encounter is actually a first for Jesus—the first encounter Mary realizes it's Jesus when he says her name; the second, it's during a sacrament; and the third, it's in his greeting. Here, it's the marks of his suffering that make it real; it's as if Jesus is saying "Thomas, I don't want you to believe in me—I want you to believe in what I did for you; I want you to look at my hands and understand my suffering."

As Thomas' heart is probably sinking as he begins to realize this, Jesus hits him a little harder by basically saying, "Shame on you for not believing."[37]

When people think of the Bible, they think about that happy ending—about Jesus rising. Who wouldn't celebrate that! But when you think about the forty days, there aren't a lot of happy endings. There's no happy ending here. The chapter ends and Thomas doesn't get a final hug it up with Jesus.

In the last chapter of the book, we'll see what happened to each of the disciples. Thomas may have not gotten his happy ending in John, but he was definitely on fire for God.

# # #

Stigmatastic!

---

[37] John 20:29: "Because you have seen me, you have believed; blessed are those who have not seen and yet have believed." (NIV)

People have been forever fascinated with the wounds on Christ's hands.

In Galatians 6:17, Paul says, "I bear on my body the marks of Jesus." Interpretation? He was probably beaten pretty badly. He uses a Greek word to describe it: Stigmata. The meaning of that word is linked to a marking or tattoo.

If the word "stigmata" sounds even a little familiar to you, then you might be a Catholic. This has become the term used to describe a Christian who has some kind of bodily mark or sore in the place that Jesus would have had his nails.

Francis of Assisi—a Catholic friar—gets credit for being the first person to ever record this phenomenon. It happened in 1224. He would not be the last. Throughout history, several people have experienced stigmata.

The last notable case was Padre Pio.

Unlike Assisi, who didn't live in a time when these sorts of things could be examined and further debunked, Pio died in 1968. Doctors examined him—some even taking X-rays. They couldn't figure it out. It was unexplained.

The marks stayed with him for 50 years. What else could have caused this? Some have speculated carbolic acid, which Pio did make a request for; but this was commonly used for sterilization, and Pio frequently administer injections to children to fight off the Spanish flu.

After 50 years, Pio died; they came for his body, and guess what they found? Or perhaps I should say, guess what they didn't find? The stigmata. It had completely disappeared.

Jesus didn't want Thomas to believe just because. He doesn't want any of us to. If a person grows up never learning about God, Jesus isn't going to stand before them and say, "How dare you for not believing! Shame on you!" Blind belief wasn't Thomas' folly.

Thomas' folly was that he heard the witness of the other disciples and he didn't believe. He got comfortable.

God puts opportunities in front of us all the time. And we make excuses. That's what Thomas did. He was given the opportunity to believe, and he said, "You know what? I'm good! If God wanted me to do this, he would have come to me too."

God, as it turned out, did come to Thomas. And it hurt. He came to him and said, "Thomas, I did tell you to do this! And you didn't do it."

God loves us. He forgives us. But when he gives you an opportunity—when he gives you witness and says, "Here it is all laid out" and you don't take it—he's going to come knocking.

Jesus didn't come to Thomas and say, "Because you didn't believe, I'm giving you cancer, or I'm taking your first child, or any other afflictions." Jesus came to Thomas and said: I'm disappointed in you.

The moral of the story isn't to show a happy ending. It's to show we can, and do, disappoint God. Disappointment is an emotional punishment that stays with us and makes us not want to do that again.

I misbehaved as a child. My parents, though they regret this now, would bring out the hand and bring on the spanking. They regret it because it didn't work. What they realized was if you want to correct the behavior of a child, then you have to affect them on an emotional level, not a physical level. A spanking stings—for a few seconds. And then it goes away.

I kept on misbehaving because it was worth it. It was worth those few seconds of sting for the glory of being a brat. But when my parents started using a different tactic—when they started saying what you are doing is disappointing us—then my behavior started to change. I didn't want to misbehave because letting someone down is far worse than the sting of a physical swat.

I would love to read Thomas' memoir, because I know this chapter of his book is the one that defined his life. I imagine it's something he talked about his entire ministry; he would probably preach multiple sermons about picking convenience and comfort over living for God. About how comfort gave him temporary happiness, but not fulfillment.

The disciples weren't chosen because they were great people; they were chosen for being ordinary people. They were chosen because a part of us lives in them. They had the same doubts that we would have had. They had the same flaws that we would have had. He picked them to show you that if they can do extraordinary things, then we can as well.

Jesus is turning these men into unstoppable Christians. When we let God into our hearts—when we invite him in and do more than just say that we believe—when we act on the belief—then we become unstoppable ourselves.

UNSTOPPABLE CHRISTIANS

Doubt happens. It happened to Thomas. It happens to all of us. Unless you happen to be so on fire—so unstoppable—that you just don't have time to do it. Robert Murray M'Cheyne was of the doubtless variety.

M'Cheyne wasn't the showy type—he didn't want his dear old mom to brag about him knowing the alphabet by the age of four. Any child could learn that. He took it up a step and learned the Greek alphabet. By 14, he was already in college. And by 18, he was ready to begin his career. He was obviously a whiz kid, but he also loved Jesus and decided to become a minister.

M'Cheyne, in addition to being a pastor, also was a poet and writer; he helped launch several mission efforts; and he created one of the most widely used systems at the time for reading the Bible (following it, people would read the New Testament and Psalms twice a year, and the Old Testament once). It sounds like a very full life, right? It was…right up until his death at the age of 29.

In the short time between graduating college at 18 and his death at 29, M'Cheyne accomplished more than most Christians can say they've accomplished in their entire life.

Doubt can be good. It can even help you grow. But it can almost limit your abilities to spread the Gospel, which is what we are called to do, and that is when doubt can become dangerous.

FIVE

THE SEA OF PETER

I like going to New York. It's not exactly exotic, but when I'm there, I get to pretend I'm someone I'm not. I get to get lost in the big city. See the sites. Eat like a local. Take in all the atmosphere. When I'm there, it's like home doesn't even exist. Home is New York.

When I go to New York—or take any vacation for that matter—work doesn't follow me. For a few short days, I can see what life would be like without it.

But I do have a home. And when I get back, I'm often overwhelmed with disappointment. Reality sinks in. Responsibilities are back. The dogs are back. The cats are back. Chores are back. My work life returns. It's like something magical had happened, but then I realize it was all just a dream—I realize the vacation is over.

The disciples had just been on an adventure. They had spent years with Jesus Christ—God in the flesh. And the icing on the cake was that he came back from the dead! It seems like they've had their great awakening. How do you go back to normal after something like that? How does life just go on?

Jesus is going to show us what happens next—what happens after we receive him? How does life just go on?

It's in our nature to forget the value of even the impactful things.[38]

Jesus appeared to the disciples, and then life went on. John doesn't record how long it took for life to go on, but in 21:2, it says that Simon Peter said, "I'm going fishing," and a few of the other disciples went with him. It seems odd at first, but fishing is what they knew. It was their job. It was their way of making life go on.

The thing to understand here is that seeing Jesus doesn't make you live for Jesus—it doesn't make you have a relationship with him, and it surely doesn't give you salvation. If you look up from this book and there in front of you is Jesus Christ, and he's going in for a high five: you don't automatically get marked as a disciple of Christ. You're marked as being a witness to something miraculous, but that's about it.

The fact that these disciples had followed Jesus for all those years—the fact that they saw him—none of that gives them salvation. They are certainly on the path, but they still

---

[38] How many people remember the 2002 Nord-Ost Siege? You should…over 150 people died and nearly 900 were taken hostage. "But that wasn't on American soil, so why should I remember it?" you say? Fine. How about Emmett Till? See how many of your friends remember him. He's the 14-year-old who was lynched in 1955 for "supposedly" flirting with a white woman. The men who murdered him were acquitted of the crime.

don't know what it means to have the personal relationship with Jesus that he came to bring.

So, it should not be surprising at all that they're fishing; they're just doing what they thought they were expected to do. But they weren't doing it very well. They didn't catch a single fish.

When Jesus shows up on the shore and calls out to them, it's back to the drawing board—his beloved disciples again have absolutely no idea who it is.

After a formal greeting, Jesus instructs them to toss their net to the right of the boat if they want to catch fish. (John 21:6) Not knowing this was Jesus, it wouldn't have been odd for them to reject the advice. But they followed—perhaps as an act of desperation. And when they did, they caught so many fish, they weren't even able to haul up their net.

It almost seems like a jerk move; one moment they can't catch any fish and the next they are catching so many fish they can't even bring up their net—these guys are losing even when they're winning! But there's a parable going on. This net is exactly what the road ahead will look like—they will become missionaries, and when they follow the instructions of God, their nets will be full of believers.

In Luke 5:10, Jesus has just performed a very similar miracle when he calls his first disciples and he tells Peter, "Don't be afraid, from now on you will fish for people." Peter no doubt remembers this miracle, and will eventually see the connection and understand that this man on the edge of the sea is Jesus.

The Bible is full of bookends—stories that come around full circle and complete perfectly. In Matthew 4:18-19, Jesus stands beside the Sea of Galilee and he calls two of his disciples, Peter and Andrew. And here we are again. Jesus stands beside the Sea of Galilee and he's about to ask his disciples to take the next step—not just to follow him, but to spread his name to the world. It's fitting.

And it's this bookend, full-circle story that perhaps makes Peter jump in the water; Peter was able to walk on water the first time. That's not the case here, but it's interesting that John takes note of who saw Jesus first—John did.[39] Peter is full of energy and passion, but John appears to be the thinker of the group. And Jesus loves them both equally.

While Peter is throwing all his passion into getting to Jesus as quick as humanly possible, John and others are towing in the net full of fish. When you look at the church, you see all sorts, and none are better than the others—they all are needed to make the church work. Peter is the charismatic one who expresses his faith more outwardly at times than others—and you need that. But then you have John, and he's on the boat realizing that they need people to stay with the boat or they'll lose all this food they just caught.

When they arrive on shore, they see that there's already a fire burning and food waiting. Jesus is showing once again that he's still a servant. He's did something truly remarkable and it would be hard to blame him if he stood on the shore with his arms in the air shouting "Worship me!" But he's

---

[39] John 21:7

showing the disciples that even in his resurrected state that he is a servant. He's giving them an example to follow.

All this begs the question: why the fish? Why did he help them catch all this fish when he already had a feast prepared? Maybe Jesus caught the "what gives?" look on their face because in verse 10 he says, "Bring some of the fish you have just caught." Jesus may have gotten the dinner started, but this is going to be a shared feast.

The passion (and muscle) of Peter shows again because he went right to the fish and carried it to Jesus all by himself. Peter is trying desperately to impress Jesus—and he should be—he is, after all, the guy who completely denied knowing Jesus just a few days before; he's obviously overjoyed to see Jesus, but probably also a little terrified—and definitely still full of guilt.

Let's think about this image for just a minute. Peter singlehandedly carries this giant haul of fish. It doesn't say what kind of fish this is, but let's just assume it is one of the most common breeds of fish found in the Sea of Galilee: The Galilaea Tilapia. This particular fish has a maximum weight of about 3.5 pounds. But let's be conservative here; let's just say the fish are 2 pounds on average. That's over 300 pounds of fish that Peter is singlehandedly carrying. That's a lot of guilt that Peter's carrying to be able to muster that kind of strength.

So, here they all are—reunited and it feels so good—except it doesn't. Things are still a bit off. Jesus invites them to eat breakfast with him, and then it goes on to say in verse 12 that none of the disciples "dared ask him, 'Who are you?' They knew it was the Lord." (NIV) Of course it's Jesus! So why does John make it sound so odd that they didn't want to ask who he was? The Bible never explains what Jesus looked like, but John and other authors certainly imply that the resurrected appearance of Jesus was different than the pre-resurrected state. Jesus is not a ghost, but he is not human either—he comes and goes as he pleases.

Jesus again takes the servant role and in verse 13, serves them bread and fish. The disciples probably feel rock bottom right about now. A few chapters back, in John 18, Peter had denied knowing Christ and in John 18:18, right after his denial, it says, "Now the servants[a] and officers had made a charcoal fire, because it was cold, and they were standing and warming themselves. Peter also was with them, standing and warming himself." You have to imagine Peter is staring at that fire and he knows what he did—the guilt inside him is probably burning hotter than those flames. And Thomas is there too—and he knew what he did. They all had denied Jesus in one way or another—and yet Jesus still serves them.

There were probably rivers of tears that night.

\# # #

When breakfast is over, Jesus moves on to the main course: Peter. He knows what Peter is going through, but he doesn't say "There, there, Peter—I forgive you. It's ok." He says bluntly in John 21:15, "Simon son of John, do you love me more than these?" (NIV) It's a hard question to hear, but perhaps made worse by the fact that he's calling him "Simon" and not "Peter." Peter means rock. Peter is meant to be the rock—the foundation—that God builds his church on. Jesus is essentially saying that Peter is not that rock…yet.

Peter had previously said he loved Jesus more than the other disciples. But what about now? It should also be noted that Jesus asks the question and uses the Greek word for love "*agapas*"—but when Peter answers that yes, of course he loves him, he uses the Greek word "*phileo*." Both are interpreted as "Love," but one is the giving, unselfish love and the other is the friendly love. So, Jesus is saying, "Peter, do you love me unselfishly?" And Peter replies by saying he loves Jesus like a friend. It's easy to see that Peter is a little more reserved and not so passionate now; he's embarrassed to say he loves Jesus like he did before because he was such a big letdown.

Jesus replies by telling Peter to "Feed my lambs." (Verse 15); the word "my" should be noted here. Jesus is not giving Peter his lambs—he's telling him to take care of them. To tend them.

Jesus asks Peter again if he loves him, and then a third time. And this third time, it really sinks in. Peter denied Jesus three times, and now Jesus is asking if he loves him three times.

Jesus gets Peter fired up, and then he leaves him with two final words: "Follow me!" (Verse 19)

You can't help but wonder what you would reply if Jesus came to you and said, "Follow me." Peter's reply is both comical and relatable. Instead of jumping up and saying, "Heck yeah, I'll follow you!" Peter almost seems downright annoyed and childish! He turns to John and in verse 21 and gives the reply that any 5-year-old gives when they don't like what has been said: "What about him?"

Everyone who's a Christian wants to *believe* that they are on fire for Jesus, but the reality is we're human. When God calls you into action, he knows you are human. Peter needs to process what's been said. It's not an instant call to action—at least for him. Yes, Peter goes on to be the shepherd to the early church—the rock that Jesus predicted he'd become. But first, he needs to digest everything and grow.

Jesus could have smacked him upside the head and said, "Really, Peter?! Grow up!" But he's gentler. In verse 22, he says, "If I want him to remain alive until I return, what is that to you? You must follow me." Jesus is saying "mind your own business"—but he's saying more than that. He's saying every believer has a different destiny. Peter was a competitive guy, but Jesus is trying to humble him. He's showing him that it's not a competition—we are all unique—we all have different paths to God.

It's also important to consider "*You* must follow me." Jesus is telling Peter that it's not about John's decision or Thomas' decision, or anyone else's decision. He can't decide if he's going to follow based on what happens to the next guy. He has to decide because it's a personal choice based solely on his relationship with Jesus Christ. This is telling for all of us. We can't look at other believers to decide if there is a God and if we want to have a relationship with us—we can only examine our own personal relationship and what God has done in our lives.

# # #

Jesus is done with his teaching to Peter, but John records more. John gives us a nugget of insight into early Christians in verse 23, "the rumor spread among the believers that this disciple would not die. But Jesus did not say that he would not die." We often look to the Bible and say, "Man, the world would be so much better if people would prescribe to the same moral code they did back then." That's not true. Reality check: people were just as messed up back then as they are today! Perhaps more so! People loved to gossip and add things to the testimony of Christ that simply were not true.

John also tells us in verse 25 there's so much more that happened that isn't in this book—that this was not Jesus' only appearance. For John, for all the disciples and gospel writers, it's the testimony that Christ brought that's important—not the acts that followed when he resurrected. The Resurrection only confirmed that the testimony is true, and so John didn't want to add special emphasis to it.

All of this happened when the disciples were doing their ordinary work. That's important. It's not when they are in this reflective, monastic state that all of this happens. God is showing us that he changed people who were just like you and me. You don't have to go to church to find God—he'll find you, and he'll find you in the place that you normally dwell.

Unstoppable Christian

Jesus used Peter, in part, to illustrate a concept completely foreign to Jews at the time: Grace. Peter messed up—he messed up in the worst possible way. As a good Jew, Peter felt bad, no doubt, and probably felt it was high time to get thee to the alter and sacrifice a lamb. But he was in for a surprise: a lamb couldn't save him. There were no sacrifices he himself could make. There was nothing Peter could do to be forgiven…except accept Jesus Christ and receive the grace that he freely offers.

Grace was a foreign idea to Peter. It's foreign to many of us. And it's been one of the most difficult concepts for many Christians to fully understand…which brings us to another Peter: Peter Damian.

Peter was born to a noble family about 1007; noble they were, rich they were not. Though he had a nice noble name, he did not have a nice childhood. Still he overcame, and before his 30th birthday he was already a famous teacher of theology.

While riding high in academia, he decided that this kind of lifestyle just gave him too many luxuries; he left the university where he taught and entered a life of solitude. He was essentially a hermit.

Damian, however, wasn't known for being a smart guy who became a hermit. Few would probably take note if that was the case. Damian was known for being the father of Christian flagellation.

Flagellation, for those unfamiliar, is essentially whipping or lashing someone (including yourself). Damian came up with this idea that we could be a whole lot more devoted if we tortured ourselves. If Peter the apostle was one of his students, then grace wouldn't have brought him closer to God—a good lashing would.

Damian was devoted. Unstoppable, even. He left everything. He could have had a lavish lifestyle, but he chose instead to be a hermit. He understood grace, and yet he still felt that grace wasn't enough, that true devotion meant having to put yourself through torture. He was a wise man, and yet his wisdom could not bring him to see that no lashing could bring him closer to God. You cannot control sin with a whip. Prayer, yes. Meditation, yes. Learning, even. But if you are trying to become better through a beating, then you probably took one too many beatings to the head because it's not going to happen.

SIX

WHAT'S SO GREAT ABOUT A COMMISSION

You've seen the opening acts, now it's time to get to the main attraction. Because when it comes down to it, the Resurrection wasn't about doing a flashy miracle; it wasn't about proving Jesus Christ was Messiah; and it wasn't to convince people to believe. It certainly did all of these things. But the Resurrection was really about Jesus giving his final teaching before assuming his place in Heaven.

The most detailed account of the Great Commission is in Matthew. In fact, aside from giving an account of the Resurrection, this is the only post-Resurrection event Matthew records. For his Gospel—for the people he was witnessing to—what transpired at the Great Commission was the single most important lesson for them to understand.

Matthew 28:16 tells us the 11 made their way to Galilee; the Bible doesn't reveal a lot about why. Did Jesus tell them in one of his appearances to get up there? Or are they finally starting to believe what Jesus told them before he died? If you need a refresher, Jesus said prior to his death that he would go to Galilee (see Matthew 26:32 and Mark 14:28). We don't even know at what mountain all of this appeared at. But none of that is important.

So, what's important? What is it that Matthew wants his reader to know? And in turn, what does Jesus want us to know? In a nutshell: that the disciples were there together. All 11 of them. Because this isn't a teaching Jesus is giving his all-star lineup—this is something they're getting as a group. That's important. The Great Commission isn't something for individual believers—it's something for all believers.

What a relief, right?! They're there together and they've finally come to terms with all of this being real! Awesome! Radical! Wrong. Because, while they did go there together, verse 17 tells us that "some doubted"! What's more, "they worshiped him; but some doubted." They worshiped him even when they doubted him! Who are these people?! Us. That's who they are.

The disciples really do represent us because that's how a lot of people would be if Jesus came today. They'd bow to the crown in worship on the outside, but still doubt on the inside. They're seeing a man come back from the dead: and they're still doubting!

It doesn't say who the "some" were, but the author wants us to know that it happened. He wants us to know that a human experience happened during a holy encounter. He wants us to know that it's ok to have doubts. The reality is, God doesn't want us to believe blindly—he wants us to look at a supernatural experience and make sure what we are seeing is of God and not of something else.

Still, Mark's account of the event (Mark 16:14-18) tells us that Jesus didn't go softly on them for their unbelief. God is patient with us, but there comes a point where we have all the evidence and we either have to take it and believe or not believe. In verse 14, it says "He rebuked them for their lack of faith and their stubborn refusal to believe those who had seen him after he had risen." (NIV)

God can use even our unbelief to his glory, because this unbelief tells us something: that there was no conspiracy. People who argue that the disciples essentially hid his body and made up a story of the Resurrection should take note here, because the Bible is essentially telling us that even the disciples—the ones who followed him and left everything for his teachings—did not expect this Resurrection and, in many ways, didn't want to even believe in it. Why conspire to do something they did not believe was possible? Had they conspired then this scene would have looked differently; the disciples wouldn't have been so confused because they expected everything—they were the ones writing the history. But that wasn't the case.

Unlike the other teachings Jesus has given, this one isn't so much a teaching than a command. The disciples had probably come to expect Jesus to mysteriously show up and tell them more things to increase their faith, but he's all done with that. His time on Earth has come to an end and he's all done trying to convince them and teach them. The only teaching he gives is Matthew 28:18: "All authority in Heaven and on earth has been given to me." (NIV)

For those who say that Jesus never said he was God, they're right. He didn't say he was God…not in that exact phrasing, that is. He said it in so many other ways, however. This verse is one example. He's telling the disciples that he has complete and total authority in both Heaven and Earth. Mere men do not make this claim. He's telling his disciples that he is God and he has the authority to say what he's about to say.

And with that final teaching, he moves on and gives them a direct command:

> Therefore, go and make disciples of all nations, baptizing them in the name of the Father and of the Son and of the Holy Spirit, and teaching them to obey everything I have commanded you. And surely, I am with you always, to the very end of the age." (Matthew 28:19-20, NIV)

This verse is weighted! First, "Therefore, go and make disciples of all nations." Some translations, such as the KJV, say "teach all nations." Both mean the same thing, but "teach" might help make it more understandable for some, because what Jesus is saying here is that the disciples are no longer students—they are teachers. He's told them what they needed to know and now it's going to be on them to tell the world about them. And that brings us to the second important point, "nation."[40] Because Jesus is instructing them not to tell Jews about him, but *everyone* about him. God has just been unleashed to the world. The first covenant was between him and

[40] Or world.

his chosen people, but in his second covenant we are all his chosen people.

Mark 16:15 also gives this special emphasis to preach the Gospel to Jews and Gentiles alike when he says, "Go into all the world and preach the gospel to all creation." It may seem easy to follow today, but is it really? Because there are people who you probably hide the Gospel from—maybe because you don't think they'll care? Maybe because you are embarrassed that they know you are a believer? Or maybe because you're afraid that they'll throw insults at you or challenge your faith? God does not like excuses. He's very clear here. You should preach his Gospel everywhere and to everybody—create possibilities for sharing your belief in all that you do.

Jesus continues, "…baptizing them in the name of the Father and of the Son and of the Holy Spirit" (NIV). Baptizing is important here, but more important is that second part: "name of the Father and of the Son and of the Holy Spirit." That's obviously a reference to the Trinity, but what's more: that's the first time the Trinity is ever recorded in the Bible; prior to this, the Father, Son and Holy Spirit had all been referenced in the Bible, but never together.

To put what's going on here into a little bit more context, let's go to 1 Corinthians 10:2, Paul writes that under the Old Covenant, the Jewish people were "all baptized into Moses in the cloud and in the sea." So, what Paul is saying is when a person is baptized they are essentially adopting that person as their teacher; what Jesus is saying here—commanding here—is that this old system is gone; under the New Covenant, a person is baptized and receives God as their teacher.

But why not just say, "Baptizing in the name of God"? It proves that the union is equal—Father is not greater than Son is not greater than Spirit.

Mark 16:16 adds a bit more to baptism: condemnations. "Whoever believes and is baptized will be saved, but whoever does not believe will be condemned." (NIV)

Jesus doesn't say this as a command—to go and condemn the world. He says it as a warning. Your family members who don't believe will be condemned; so will your friends; and co-workers. Everyone. Save them!

Jesus doesn't say that people who don't believe "are condemned." He says they "will be." There's a chance to save them. He says this to put urgency on the situation. Not to wait for the right opportunity, but to make every opportunity right.

So far, Christ has said in this verse his disciples are first to go out and convert, and then they are to baptize; in the next verse, he commands them to teach: "teaching them to obey everything I have commanded you." There's a word in there you should pay close attention to: I. "Everything *I* have commanded you." Jesus is telling them, they are not the judges. They don't make the law. They don't make the teachings. They teach what he has taught.

It's easy to tell people what we believe God wants others to do—how we believe he wants them to act and command. But that's not Biblical. That's not what we are commanded to do. We are commanded only to teach what Christ has taught, which we can read in the Gospels.

Finally, Christ ends with a promise: "And surely, I am with you always, to the very end of the age." (NIV) Christ's body is leaving Earth, but his spirit will dwell on the Earth as long as there are still Christians on Earth—he is protecting us, holding us up and encouraging us, and blessing us. *But* there will come an end to this age. We can't predict when this will come, nor should we predict. Christ tells us this for the same reason he has always mentioned that we don't know when the end will come—we must seize the day while we still can.

In a nutshell, the Great Commission is Christ first asserting his power and authority over all believers; he authorizes his disciples to use this authority, and finally he gives a promise.

The Great Commission is often associated with missionaries—the people called to go out and spread the messages to the corners of the world who have never heard of Christ or who don't have the resources to be taught. It's fitting, so why not use it? But the Great Commission isn't a call for missionaries. It's a call for us. It's a call for community. It's God showing us that we are one people—one church—in Christ. So far, Christ has come to the women, to the strangers, to the disciples, to the doubters, and to the leaders—now he comes to the community of believers. His teachings are spreading larger and larger; each appearance reaches a larger group.

But Mark 16:17-18 gives us just a little bit more:

> And these signs will accompany those who believe: In my name, they will drive out demons; they will speak in new tongues; they will pick up snakes with their hands; and when they drink deadly poison, it will not hurt them at all; they will place their hands on sick people, and they will get well. (NIV)

There should be a few things noted about this passage. First, Jesus does not say if these things will happen for a short time or for all time. Second, it does not say everyone will have these gifts.

But let's talk about the bigger elephant in the room. There are some wacky things going on here: snake handling! Drinking poison?! How are we supposed to read this? What is the takeaway? Should we be bringing cobra snakes to church on Sunday? Should we put poison in the communion cup and just see what happens?

Pull out your Bibles. Got them? Now go ahead and read through the entire New Testament and find all the instances of people getting bit by snakes and drinking poison. Got them all. Now, let's count them up. Feel free to use just one hand; heck go ahead and just use one finger! Because there's only one instance of it.

Acts 28:3-4 tells the story of a viper jumping out at Paul, but that Paul is not harmed by the venom.

If this is supposed to be a common thing, then it would be all over the place in the Bible. Snakes jumping up in every chapter!

What gives? Why is Jesus telling it? It's not to get people excited. It's to give them an illustration. We aren't supposed to test God by taming snakes and drinking poison. But Jesus is showing that God will do these miraculous things for his glory—that when we see them happen, we can say they are from God.[41] They will happen if it is necessary to show that God protects his people.

# # #

God is unleashed to the community of believers in the Great Commission—nothing can stop them from getting God's message across; God will use any means to protect his community to bring that message to the unsaved. It's fitting that this last teaching gives one of the most important lessons: we aren't in this alone. We are a body of believers.

What made the disciplines grow and become unstoppable—what makes us unstoppable as believers—is knowing that we aren't in it alone. God will never ask or expect you to do anything without the support of other Christians. It may certainly feel that way at times, but if you are ever truly alone, then you should evaluate why. We have fellowship in Christ, and we have fellowship with each other.

UNSTOPPABLE CHRISTIANS

When Jesus said we should go forth and make disciples of men (Matthew 28:19), it's easy to see it as more of the closing line to a great movie. Inspiring. But it's not based on a real story, right? We aren't supposed to actually do that, are we? We're just supposed to be happy and be nice to people, right?

---

[41] So leave your snakes at home!

Because the reality is, as Christians—as humans—it's easy to become a Christian and get...comfortable. To turn the Great Commission into the Great "Let's Do Our Best to Support Missionaries Financially...Unless That's a Burden Too...At Which Point We'll Just Say We'll Keep Them in Thoughts and Prayers."[42] If we're being honest, the Great Commission is easier to read than to actually do...unless you are Amy Carmichael.

Born in 1867, Amy suffered from neuralgia.[43] It wasn't a life-ending illness, but it was enough to get you a pass when God was handing out "Who's Going to Be a Missionary?" cards. But Amy pushed forward and accepted a call to go to Asia. While in Japan, she fell ill and was sent home, but made a detour in India. She never returned home. She stayed and served India for over 50 years without a single furlough.

At the time, India had a custom of forcing children[44] into prostitution at Hindu temples; Hindu priests would serve as pimps and collect the money. Amy created a ministry to rescue the girls.

Her illness forced her to become bedridden for the last two decades of her life, but she remained in India

---

[42] And *sometimes* we do keep them in our prayers.

[43] A neurological condition that makes you constantly feel achy.

[44] Notably young girls.

where she became an author of over a dozen books. Three years before her death in 1951, India outlawed temple prostitution.

SEVEN

OTHER APPEARANCES

In terms of college slackers, I was as nerdy as they come. I would often ditch classes because I was in some dusty corner of the campus library reading—everything from reference books to theses from former students. I'm not entirely sure how I passed, but that's beside the point. The point is, while I was in one of these dusty corners, I came across the Christian history section and found books I'd never heard of before: apocryphal works of the New Testament. It was enough alternative history to make Dan Brown pass out in utter joy.

There was nothing secret about any of these books. They may not have been talked about in Sunday school, but they were certainly talked about everywhere else—for hundreds of years.

It's taken six chapters to get to the epic conclusion of Jesus' final time on Earth. But before getting to the closing act, there are a few more non-Gospel events that are worth examining.

Leave on a cable history channel long enough, and you'll be bound to see more than your fair share of stories about what the church doesn't want you to know. And what is it that the church doesn't want you to know? That Jesus had a twin brother, that Jesus was married, that Jesus fought dragons, the list goes on and on.

TV shows have it right. Sort of. Because these events, and more, are things referenced in books outside the Bible. What they have wrong is that they say these books are hidden from us. They are not. The books have been known for centuries. There's nothing remotely hidden about them.

The reason they aren't in the Bible isn't because of their content. If Jesus was a dragon master, trust me, you'd know! The reason is because the works that they come from are simply too late to be considered authoritative.

Think of it like this. You're studying the history of the Revolutionary War and some guy stands up and says, "Look, there's something you don't know about the war. My family has passed down secret knowledge of this war for over 200 years, and my great, great, great, great, great grandpa said George Washington crafted a gun out of his shoe." I guess that could have happened. But you won't see that added to history books anytime soon—not because it's a strange story, but because it can't be verified.

So, what are we to do? Chalk the stories up as heresy and never speak of them again? Of course not! For two reasons. One, they might be true. Two, even if they aren't true, they surely teach us about the thought process of early Christians.

There are two stories of note that tell us something about the forty days.

\# # #

The first is The Gospel of Hebrews. Some apocryphal works are...bizarre; others might have been included in the Bible had they actually been available. The Gospel of Hebrews belongs to that second group. The book was so well-loved that it was quoted by several early church fathers. Why wasn't it included in the Bible? One of the biggest things going against it is that only fragments exist. There's no complete work available anywhere.

The Gospel reiterates what several of the New Testament gospels say, but it has one key passage that's not: a resurrection appearance to James, the Brother of Jesus:

> And when the Lord had given the linen cloth to the servant of the priest, he went to James and appeared to him. For James had sworn that he would not eat bread from that hour in which he had drunk the cup of the Lord until he should see him risen from among them that sleep. And shortly thereafter the Lord said: Bring a table and bread! And immediately it is added: He took the bread, blessed it and broke it and gave it to James the Just and said to him: My brother, eat thy bread, for the Son of man is risen from among them that sleep.

What should we make of that? First, who is James? Was he a "brother" of Christ in the literal sense or the figurative?[45] Catholics and Orthodox Christians would agree in the figurative—Mary, according to them, was a virgin for life-er. Most Protestants, however, are a little more open to James as a

---

[45] "Fist bumps to my homie" sense.

literal brother. In the case of the family variety, it makes more sense why Jesus might appear to James—it could have merely been because he was a disciple, but it also could have been because he needed to appear to family and give closure.

Family matters aside, what insight can the encounter offer us? It gives us a slightly different take on the Upper Room; unlike the other Gospel accounts, James believes in the Resurrection before it actually happens.

Mary and the Case of Perpetual Virginity

Cover your eyes, young children, because I'm about to ask one of the most pressing early theological questions of the church—one that people still ask today: Did Mary have sex?

If you err on the side of, "Is that really a thing? I thought she married Joseph and had lots of happy children?" Then you're probably wondering what gives with that whole virgin for life thing. So…what gives?

The New Testament does, of course, talk about Jesus having brothers, but those verses could mean half-brothers or more spiritual brothers. The doctrine of perpetual virginity didn't really kick into high gear until after all the apostles had died; one of the first cases for it is in an apocryphal work known as the *Protoevangelium of James*.

If you believe in the doctrine of virgin 'til death, that's likely based on how you view Mary. Is Mary just Mary, or to carry the child of God, doesn't she have to be holier than that? Fans of the doctrine essentially believe that Mary represented the faithful spouse to the Holy Spirit who impregnated her—having relations with her Earthly husband meant she was cheating on the Spirit. Cheating may have been the case *before* birth, but after birth the question is whether or not she was still married to the Holy Spirit in the absolute literal sense.

The Catholic and Orthodox Churches aren't without their fair argument—translators have argued with valid points both for and against the perpetual virginity. The importance of their argument can extend into another theological belief they hold as true: the assumption of Mary. Contrary to what some believe, assumption doesn't mean she was taken away before she died (though some hold that to be the case). What does it mean? Well nobody likes to be a Debbie downer, but many Christians believe we don't go to Heaven when we die—we go there when Christ returns for us. We're essentially just chilling in our graves. There's certainly room to disagree here, but, fret not, it's not like you'll be bored out of your mind in a coffin—you won't even know you've been dead. But if you believe in the assumption of Mary, then basically you believe that we die and wait, but Mary didn't have to wait—she was taken straight away to Heaven; for that to happen, however, they hold she would have had to remain pure and not have sexual relations.

While not having sex with Joseph would certainly make Mary devoted, the question you really have to ask is: does it matter?

The Gospel of Bartholomew doesn't mess around when it comes to the Resurrection; unlike the Gospels, which spend pretty much the entire account talking about Jesus' teaching, Bartholomew gets right to the Resurrection—and then he gets to hell.

In his account,[46] Jesus is almost like an action hero—he's on a mission from God, he's in hell, and it's payback time. It has all the makings of an epic—angels, torture, and, of course, Bible heroes like Adam.

What the account doesn't have is much truth. The theme of predestination is a big one in the book.

---

[46] And by his, I mean some other guy because this was certainly not written by Bartholomew, the apostle—it was written hundreds of years after.

Jesus goes to hell again in another apocryphal work, the Gospel of Nicodemus—this time he even manhandles Satan and turns him over to be tortured. The account, like that of Bartholomew, is hundreds of years after the fact. Both of these stories have been deemed Gnostic accounts.

What's a Gnostic you may ask?

Luke 1:1 gives us our first clues about this wacky thing known as Gnosticism. He writes, "Many have undertaken to draw up an account of the things that have been fulfilled among us." (NIV) Luke could be referencing other Gospel writers, but the word "many" might also mean more people than just the Gospel writers have taken to writing accounts; and the fact that he's careful to point out that his will be more historical implies the others maybe have been not so truthful.

That's a lot of maybes. Let's get to the certainties of the Gnostics.

Gnostics believed they possessed a secret knowledge of God. They would make up outlandishly bizarre stories and say it was true because God told it just to them. Mormons could certainly fall into this territory, because their entire religion is based on an account of a man who had a secret revelation from God.

Luke's Gnostics were probably not quite as crazy; they were likely just people who got bad accounts of a story. The wackier Gnostics started popping up in the second and third centuries. By this time all the eyewitnesses of Jesus had died and it made it easier for a person to pop up and make stuff up. If a person claimed to have secret knowledge earlier than this, an eyewitness could just stand up and say, "This dude is out of his mind. We were there. This definitely didn't happen." And that was that.

\#   #   #

There is one final account—albeit a Biblical one—that tells us what went on during these forty days.

In 1 Corinthians 15:6, Paul gives us a tidbit not included anywhere else in the Bible: "After that, he appeared to more than five hundred of the brothers and sisters at the same time, most of whom are still living, though some have fallen asleep." (NIV)

500! Wow! Awesome, right?! Except, doesn't Acts 1:15 say Christ appeared to 120?

Did Paul just give the gotcha moment that skeptics would swoop up and use against Christians? Sort of. Because skeptics do in fact use this as a way of saying the Bible contradicts itself.

Before you run off and join the skeptic brigade, pause for a moment and consider what's happening here.

First, there's a word in the Corinthians verse that skeptics don't like: "eita."

Like a lot of words in the Bible, there's a lot of room for interpretation when it comes to translation. The original Greek uses the word "eita" in the verse, which means "afterward" or "furthermore." So, while the quick glance reading will tell you Paul is giving a sequence of events—a timeframe of when things happened, if you will; what Paul is really giving is a sequence of eyewitness accounts that he felt important. He's not saying, "This happened and *then* this and *then* this." He's saying, "This happened and this happened and this happened."

Most scholars believe Corinthians was written before the Acts of the Apostle; so, Luke, who wrote Acts, would have likely known all about Paul and that 500 number—he was, after all, interviewing witnesses. It seems reasonable that Luke would have come just a tad bit closer to that number if they are talking about the same events.

If that 500 number isn't just Paul giving the wrong number for what should be 120, then what is the 500?

There are different ways to look at it. First you could say Luke isn't counting a lot of things into that 120 number—like women; or that there were 500 there but only 120 were what Luke would define as disciples.

But the more logical way would be that this 500 was an appearance prior to the 120 that simply is not recorded anywhere else. In Matthew 28:10 Jesus says, "Go and tell my brothers to go to Galilee; there they will see me." (NIV) Many suspect that this is when the appearance happened, but the time and place of the event really isn't important. In fact, many early church fathers believed that it happened a year after the Resurrection. It's the event that's important.

As has been said already, each New Testament writer had different audiences that they were writing to. Paul isn't writing a book to convert people like the Gospel writers were. He's writing to people who are believers, but are having a dispute within the church.

Paul writes that Jesus appeared to Peter, the 12, the 500, and to himself as well. What's he telling the church in the letter? He's giving a list of eyewitnesses who have authority over the church. He's telling them that they have people they can go to—that it isn't just these 12 little guys that they have to believe; there are literally hundreds who can give testament of the events. He's telling them that they can't just go about and make up their own gospel—nor should they have to, because there's plenty of facts out there that tell them exactly what they need to know.

We don't, unfortunately, know what happened when Jesus appeared to the 500; one can only imagine it was some teaching. But Paul wants his readers to know it. And God wants us to know it. Why? Because it helps cement the fact that these events happened. Jesus didn't appear to a handful. He appeared to over 500 at one time! It's easy to say Mary(s) were in shock and just saw what they thought was Jesus; that the disciples stole the body; that the two men walking that Jesus appeared to were simply nuts; that Paul had a seizure and saw some wacky vision; that...it's easy to keep making excuses.

500 is no longer an intimate encounter; it's a concert! It's a gathering.

God appeared to 500 because that's what he felt people needed. 500 people witnessed this. If you are going to deny it and believe that more than 500 were crazy, fine. Because if you can't believe in 500, then you won't believe in 1,000 or 10,000. God gives us enough—faith gives us the rest. You either have to submit to faith—submit to God—or just walk away because nothing is going to make you believe.

God is selective. He reveals not what we want to know, but what we need to know. That's how we should approach the forty days. We should look at what he shows us and ask, "What does God want us to know?"

Once you consider that, then you can move on to the Ascension.

UNSTOPPABLE CHRISTIAN

Some of the New Testament apocrypha was downright wacky tabacky; but every once in a while, there were stories of Christians who were unstoppable. Perpetua's life wasn't just unstoppable—it was legendary. So, legendary, in fact, that Augustine once warned Christians against making her story equal to the Bible.

Perpetua was born in the second century to a wealthy, but pagan, family; around 201 AD, when the emperor of Rome forbade conversions to Christianity. Perpetua and many others were among those rounded up. She was a brand-new Christian who was preparing to be baptized.

So, off she goes to prison, where things aren't as bad as they could have been—they let her dear old dad visit to try and convince her to renounce her faith, and even allow her to breastfeed her newly born child. When she refused to renounce her faith, she was sentenced to death in the arena.

According to legend,[47] she kept a diary of her life in prison leading up to her death and sneaked it off to another person. It became the *Diary of Anne Frank* of her day, and was read in churches for hundreds of years.

---

[47] And by legend, I mean some have argued some of this.

EIGHT

THE ASCENSION

And now we at last arrive. The moment we've all been waiting for: The Ascension.

The greatest post-Resurrection miracle is, of course, the Ascension. But why? Why was it so important for Jesus to ascend into Heaven? What happened when it happened, and what happened because it happened? Does it even matter to us today? Did it *really* matter to the disciples back then?

Let's rewind a little bit before going forward. Why did the disciples need to be at the Ascension? They weren't at his Resurrection. Why is this encounter so special? In a word: Proof.

The proof of the Resurrection is that Jesus Christ stood in front of them. Of course, he resurrected! You don't have to see the moment of resurrection to know he has been raised. But how do you prove the Ascension? They needed to be there. They needed to be eyewitnesses to the event.

But why Ascension at all?

Ephesians 4:8 tells us when Christ ascended, he led "captivity captive" (KJV)—in other words he conquered sin and death; this itself is something that Psalm 68:18 predicted;[48] in his death on the cross, Christ was sacrificing himself for all mankind. Prior to this, Jews had to offer a sacrifice for the forgiveness of sin; Christ put an end to that. But through his Resurrection and Ascension, he proved that he not only defeated sin, but he also defeated death.

Jesus promised his disciples that he would leave this Earthly world, but that he will "give you another advocate to help you and be with you forever." (John 14:16, NIV) Jesus ascends to Heaven with the promise of the Holy Spirit.

The Ascension also fulfills the promise that Jesus will return to the Father. John 16:28: "I came from the Father and entered the world; now I am leaving the world and going back to the Father."

Finally, Jesus is ascending to create a place for us. John 14:2 "if that were not so, would I have told you that I am going there to prepare a place for you?"

The Ascension meant many other things, of course. It was the symbolic conclusion of his ministry on Earth. It showed a visual path of his return to Heaven—the disciples would be able to confidently say that Christ not only rose from the dead, but that he dwells in Heaven. It marks the beginning of a new age—Heaven opened up and will reopen when he returns to Earth.

---

[48] "You have ascended on high, you have led captivity captive." (NIV)

Jewish Sacrifice

Jews no longer make alter sacrifices because their temple was destroyed in 70 AD; the numerologist fan inside me will point out that Jesus died in either 30 AD or 33 AD; scholars have argued both dates, but if we date his death at 30 AD and the temple was destroyed in 70 AD, then that's a forty year gap—forty day gap between the Resurrection and Ascension; forty year gap between the Resurrection and complete end of temple sacrifice.

But what's the deal with sacrifice anyway? If you need a quick refresher, when God established a covenant with the people of Israel; Jews would offer a sacrifice—sometimes, but not always, an animal—as atonement for sin. Christians believe Jesus established a new covenant not with one people, but all people, and he is the atonement for our sins.

If Jews no longer have a temple to make sacrifices in and they don't believe Christ can give them forgiveness, then how do they believe they are forgiven? The main way is Tzedakah. Tzedakah is the act of giving to those in need. Orthodox Jews still believe the temple will be rebuilt and sacrifices will resume.

# # #

If you knew you were going to die—be taken up to Heaven—what would your last words be? Your family is all gathered around you, anticipating what you might say. This is their last memory of you on Earth.

The composer Beethoven went with simple for his last words, "Friends applaud, the comedy is finished." Emily Dickinson went with a poetic, "I must go in, the fog is rising." And American frontiersman Kit Carson went with chili, "I just wish I had time for one more bowl of chili."[49]

It's with this last moment—the last words of Jesus Christ before leaving Earth—that Luke has left us. Jesus knows his forty days are up. It's time to ascend into Heaven. It's time to leave his followers with parting words. But we don't get to hear them. All this buildup and we don't even know what he said?! Sort of. Because while we don't know what he said, we know what he did. Luke says he, "lifted up his hands and blessed them."[50]

His final act on Earth was a blessing.

Stop and think about that for a second. Most people just want to get in one last word—one wise thing to be remembered by. There were words here, for sure; Mark 16:19 says, "After the Lord Jesus had spoken to them," (NIV) which clearly shows there were words. But it's the action that is remembered. In his last act, he made it about them.

What else do we know? His hands are risen. Okay. Who cares, right? But why are they risen? Two things come to mind. One, he is showing authority. But two, and perhaps more importantly, he is separated from them. When you think

---

[49] He must have really loved chili.

[50] Luke 24:50

of a blessing, what do you think about? Normally it's someone laying a hand over someone. Not so here, however. It's as if Christ is laying his hands over the entire world—not just a group of people—the blessing is radiating out—not onto specific people, but out onto the world.

The Ascension itself is pretty darn incredible. But it's not unique. Elijah ascended to Heaven. 2 Kings 2:11 says, "As they were walking along and talking together, suddenly a chariot of fire and horses of fire appeared and separated the two of them, and Elijah went up to Heaven in a whirlwind." (NIV) But this Ascension is different. Elijah needed angels. Christ went to Heaven by his own power.

Finally, both Luke and Mark tell us he didn't ascend any old place; he ascended into Heaven. Heaven is obviously important because…well, it's Heaven! But it's more than that. On Earth, he was limited by space and time. Heaven defies all the rules of Earth. Jesus is no longer bound in one physical place. He is now boundless—he can travel everywhere and to anybody—fully accessible all the time.

# # #

When you think of the Ascension, you might have a picture in your head. If you're like a lot of people, maybe it's grandiose: fireworks in the sky, flames shooting from Jesus' eyeballs, a mariachi band randomly playing in the background, because, why not? It's very human to think this way. Because when we think "God" the only thing we can think is something powerful—like Thor. But God sees larger than life differently. I'm sure God knows all about Thor, but his conception of mighty and epic is much different than yours and mine. When you think about the Ascension, try your best to get out of human mindset.

It's impossible to paint a picture of the Ascension because we weren't there and there's no accounts from eyewitnesses that describe it in detail. So, we have to guess. I imagine it wasn't as epic as my imagination might assume. It was probably simple and beautiful—a piece of the sky opening and just a tiny fragment of Heaven being revealed.

In some ways, it's interesting that he ascended at all; Heaven, after all, isn't in the sky. If you float high enough, you don't reach it. Jesus could have just as easily walked into Heaven, I suppose. But God is giving the disciples the best representation of Heaven that they knew. To these men, Heaven probably was in the sky.

The details really don't matter. The ministry matters. What follows matters.

Some have concluded that the Ascension was in fact a spiritual act—that he didn't actually ascend in the physical sense of the word. But that doesn't make sense. Think about it like this: you're at an important meeting; it's one of those meetings that can make or break you. You're just about to go in and your phone vibrates: a text from your partner, who's making the presentation with you; it reads, "I'm sorry, but I can't make it—but I'll be with you in spirit." How do you think that meeting is going to go? Do you think your partner will be with you in spirit? No! Being there in spirit does nothing for you! Maybe you do okay on the presentation, but what's going to happen when you see your partner? Are you going to high five him and say, “I couldn’t have did it if you weren’t there with me in spirit.” Absolutely not!

If Jesus had merely “spiritually” ascended, then the change that happens next to the disciples would not have happened. They saw something—they saw the physical Ascension of Jesus Christ. That’s what motivated the ministry that was about to follow them for the rest of their days on Earth.

# # #

After the Ascension, the disciples seem instantly changed. They still haven’t received the promised Holy Spirit.[51] But it says in Luke 24:52 that they worshiped him. No longer is Jesus the teacher or the prophet—this is a different kind of worship. This is the worship you give to God and to God alone.

What must be remembered about what happened next is there’s a gap. Acts continues where Luke let off, but the Holy Spirit doesn’t come after the Ascension—not right after, anyway. The disciples return to Jerusalem with the expectation of what’s to come—the promise of an advocate. And so, it’s hard not to wonder what that waiting period was like. They probably stayed near the temple worshiping God in preparation. We know how many days they waited,[52] but they did not.

The experience is something most of us sadly don’t know. Worship for most of us is the singing we do on Sundays. These guys were putting this kind of worship to shame.

I’m not sure I can fully imagine this kind of worship, but I don’t imagine something that was charismatic—disciples

[51] Spoiler alert, that’s the next chapter.

[52] FYI, 10.

dancing and singing in the streets. I think they gathered in close communion, and they prayed. I imagine it was a very intimate time as God prepared their hearts and they listened. There was probably more silence than talking—meditating on what would happen next.

When we think about Peter and John and the other all-star disciple lineup, we think of strong, courageous men; but I don't think this was the case—at least here. I think there was still a lot of fear and confusion. The disciples weren't that different than you and me—they had the greatest teacher who ever lived, but they were still men. God chose them because they were like you and me. As they worshiped, they probably were talking amongst each other about what this meant.

I used to think, if I prayed hard enough, then I could be this radical Christian—that I could go out there and speak to anyone and instantly convert them. I used to think that. God doesn't make radical Christians overnight—He makes them over time. If God were to radicalize a person, then it wouldn't be authentic—it would be forced. And God's not into forcing people into doing things. What God does instead is, He lets us change at the pace that we believe—radicalize as truth is revealed.

That's what's happening as they worship God here. He's slowly preparing them for what's going to happen next.

# # #

Jesus' death was really a seed in the ground; he died so his seed could be planted and it could rise to produce fruit.

Mark ends a little differently than Luke—not contradictory—just different. Mark 16:20 says, "Then the disciples went out and preached everywhere, and the Lord worked with them and confirmed his word by the signs that accompanied it." (NIV)

We aren't supposed to go out into the world and say that Christ rose. We're supposed to go out and prove it—show God manifested in the works and actions that we do.

Maybe you're a great debater, and you can win a person to Christianity with your words. But rarely do conversions happen during debates. They happen over actions. They happen when people look at you and say, "Something is different about that person—I want to be like that."

You can't see Christ in words—you can only hear his name and hear his deeds. But you can see Christ in love; you can see him when there's a person who is acting out of love—doing something completely out of their character.

The world doesn't need radical words—it needs radical actions. That's what's about to happen with the disciples. The world is about to see men and women go out into the world and show we are all equal—there is neither Jew nor Gentile; male or female. In Christ, we are one creation. The theology will blow people away because it's the first time they're seeing something that unites instead of divides people. It's not a message for the Jews or for the rich or the poor—it's a message for all mankind. It's a message that isn't inward but rather outward—not about finding yourself, but helping others.

In love—in their actions, not their words—they are able to prove that Christ is real.

UNSTOPPABLE CHRISTIAN

The Ascension is Christ going to Heaven and paying for our salvation. We were spiritual slaves and he saved us—he bought our freedom out of this spiritual slavery. Millions of Christians, while spiritually free, were physically chained. Amanda Smith was part of the physically chained group…but she didn't let those chains stop her from moving the kingdom of Christ forward.

Amanda Smith was born in 1837; as a child, her father would perform his daily duties as a slave, and then spend the night (sometimes not sleeping) working more hours to earn enough money to buy his family's freedom. Like pretty much every African American of her day, she had it tough, but you could easily say she had it even tougher than most—by the age of 32, she had lost two husbands and four children. To work through her grief, she became active in the African Methodist Episcopal Church.

There were plenty of good 'ol white people preaching the Gospel. But African Americans? Not so much. Smith did what few African Americans before her (and a woman on top of that) did—she went to churches and spoke in front of audiences of hundreds about Jesus Christ. It was new and even unheard of.

By the time of her death, she had opened an orphanage, traveled and preached around the world, and written a book: *An Autobiography, The Story of the Lord's Dealing with Mrs. Amanda Smith, the Colored Evangelist Containing an Account of her Life Work of Faith, and Her Travels in America, England, Ireland, Scotland, India, and Africa, as An Independent Missionary.*[53]

---

[53] The title kind of gives the entire plot away, but if you'd like to read it, it's in public domain, which means you can download it for free.

NINE

PENTECOST

I spent my childhood in school. When I graduated, I went straight to college and was back in school. When I finished that, I went to grad school where—you guessed it—I was in school.

When I finished grad school, it was eye-opening. In some ways, I wasn't prepared. I didn't know anything but school. That's kind of where the disciples are—it's been all Jesus all the time; and now that phase is over, and their next chapter is beginning. It's a scary time, but God's going to get them through it. In many ways, it's what we experience in our own life—we accept Christ and we feel instantly changed…but that's really just the beginning for us: the real fireworks begin when we start to learn what it *really* means to accept Christ.

Fifty days have now passed since the Ascension. But if you thought the Ascension was it, then you're in for a shocker, because God has yet to give his encore performance: The Pentecost.

The Ascension was Jesus ascending into Heaven; Pentecost is The Spirit descending to Earth. It ties everything together. God spent forty days teaching his disciples; he's going to spend the next few seconds unleashing himself to the world. The disciples are about to learn what it *really* means to accept Christ, and the fire that starts here will never be put out.

# # #

Easter's fun. Who doesn't like bunnies hiding eggs from kids?[54] But if you really want to celebrate something, then Pentecost might make a better case for important holiday—in terms of what happened, you might even say Pentecost is the most important holiday of all Christianity. And yet, we're lucky if we get even a single sermon on it once a year. In fact, for the majority of churchgoing Christians, Pentecost represents that time of year when the pastor says, "Hey everyone! Did you know it's Pentecost today?!" And then the pastor goes on to preach something entirely different. That's a shame.

Before we consider why this event is so important, let's think about why it happened when it did. Why not three days after the Ascension? Or 12? Those are good Biblical numbers! Heck, why not even make it happen during the Ascension itself? God's already busy opening and closing the doors of Heaven—why not just make it easy on himself and get in a two for one deal?

God can tell us for sure why he does what he does one day, but we can no doubt turn to the date and see the symbols. Namely, that this day is a holiday.

---

[54] It turns out, lots of people.

Christians have Christmas; Jews have Passover. This is one of the most important holidays for any Jew. It represents the new covenant they have with God. Pentecost is known to Jews as Shavuot; it marks the end of Passover. Some Jews traditionally hold that Shavuot is also the day that King David was born (and died).[55]

If you think that the believers just happened to be hanging out at the right place and the right time and this whole Shavuot thing is merely coincidental, then you're obviously mistaken. We may call Christians, Christian—but 2,000 years ago, Christians were Jews. They just happened to be Jews who believed that Jesus was the fulfillment of prophecy. But they still practiced things as any good Jew would. And that meant Shavuot.

Jesus said to wait when he left them. And this is the moment he told them to wait for. So, it shouldn't seem all too coincidental that God chose the day that marked the end of a festival celebrating the most sacred Old Testament covenant to mark the start of a new covenant—one not exclusive to Judaism, but open to all believers.

So, here they all are, sitting together, getting their Shavuot on, when in came "a sound from Heaven as of a rushing mighty wind." (Acts 2:2, NIV) Think about this room. This is the Upper Room that they were in with Jesus during the Last Super. It's probably not a large room and these sounds were probably bouncing all over the room. We may read this and

---

[55] So, strap yourselves in, fans of "Chase's Calendar of Events"—this day's a big one.

think, "Awe! Beautiful!" But the reality is, they were probably peeing their pants right about now. They have seen literally just about every miracle you can think of, and now this! This mighty, powerful, forceful sound crashing into the room. I can imagine all of them were at least thinking, "Now what?!"

But this whole depiction is also very descriptive. You can make things up. You can exaggerate. But this description is so detailed, it seems as if it could only have come from eyewitness accounts, and that's because it did come from eyewitness accounts.

The verse continues that this Spirit "filled the whole house." This Spirit is all-encompassing—a reoccurring theme we will now see in the New Testament. The Spirit doesn't just fill people—it fills places.

And when the sounds had filled the place, the tongues of fire came out (Verse 3); it's an odd image until you think about what fire represents; it's preparing these men and women's hearts for being filled with the Spirit of God. It's burning their hearts—melting their pride, their sin—melting all that they were—so the Spirit can dwell inside of them. The spirit doesn't dwell in the heart of a sinful man—you can't say "Spirit fill me" while you're robbing a liquor store or spewing hate at a person,[56] because your heart needs to be in the right place to receive it.

Once the Spirit encompasses them, something beautiful happens; Acts 2:4 says, "All of them were filled with the Holy

---

[56] Well you can, but it's kind of pointless.

Spirit and began to speak in other tongues as the Spirit enabled them." It's unfortunate, but the hero of this verse for many people is they spoke in tongues. Tongues can sometimes feel like the black sheep of Christianity. It's the thing that crazy Christians do. What should not be overlooked is what happens before the tongues, "they were filled with the Holy Spirit." The thing that Christ tells them to wait for has come: the very presence of God now dwells inside of them. And it dwells inside every person that believes. It's not a Peter thing. Or a John thing. Or even a disciple thing. The Spirit is with every single person and it's with them in the same exact manner. No person is greater.

God is with all of us. He's with Muslims. He's with atheists. He's with all people equally. But it's only Christians whom God dwells in—whose very Spirit is alive in them. It's not a Spirit who meets your body at the door on Sunday morning. Or a Spirit who welcomes you when you get bad news, but that you hang at the door when you go out to party. It's a Spirit that never leaves you. That's always with you.

# # #

Does Everyone Who Has a Tongue, Speak in Tongues?

What's the deal with tongues? The action sure sounds Biblical, and yet step into the wrong church today and the act of tongues can seem almost...comical. Is this like *really* a thing you're supposed to believe in? Sort of. But it depends on who you ask.

If you want to get all technical about it, then start by not referring to it as "speaking in tongues"; the clinical word is: glossolalia.[57]

Glossolalia was a thing. The Spirit has its own language, and these apostles were speaking it. But here's where it gets sticky: does it happen today?

There are certainly those who feel that it does.

But what if you aren't one of them? Well, there's evidence that it doesn't as well. One perfectly accepted theological belief is that the Gift of the Spirit was something that happened in the early church; God used to communicate his covenant with believers of the early church—to essentially give them the power to write a New Testament canon of works that was God's breath. After that was complete, there was no need to continue to give the gift to believers.

There are also those who believe it still can happen, and sometimes does, but it's not a regular occurrence.

---

[57] Which, in fairness, sounds an awful lot like something you have a few hours after eating a Doritos® Cheesy Gordita Crunch taco with "beef" from *Taco Bell*.

> Regardless of what you believe, speaking in tongues is not to be taken lightly. One of the reasons the early church got in trouble was Gnostics who tried to make up their secret teachings based on what the Spirit told them. You must prayerfully consider whether or not what you are perceiving as the Spirit is actually just a crazy person mimicking a fake language.

Onlookers are baffled by the events happening; some rationalize it in verse 13 by saying they are only drunk. But verse 6 says something interesting, "Each one heard their own language being spoken." (NIV) This might bring back fond memories of the Tower of Babel for fans of the Old Testament.

The Tower of Babel represents separation. One language, scattered. And right after this story, we hear about Abraham—the man who essentially started Judaism.

So, what's happening here? God separated the world with Judaism, but here God is returning the unity that it once had with Christianity.

Many people heard what was happening, and no doubt believed as a result. The fact that some people just passed it off as a bunch of drunks is not surprising. Some people have hardened hearts. A miracle happens in front of them and they still make excuses.

# # #

Peter takes the stage in verse 14, and he's a changed man. He's taken his place as a leader in the church and believers are turning to him to understand what happens next. He's transformed from fisher of fish to fisher of men.

He's face-to-face with Jews who believe they're all crazy, and he's now going to make his case. It doesn't give an account of who these Jews are, but it's not hard to imagine that these are the very Jews who persecuted Jesus. These are the people who shouted "crucify him" less than two months ago. These are the people who are probably looking for an excuse to kill Peter himself. Verse 14 says that Peter "raised his voice"—he was a man of confidence. The man who had betrayed Jesus to save his life is now speaking up boldly as if his own life doesn't matter.[58]

He's not only speaking boldly, he's speaking Biblically. He's speaking Joel. Good little Jewish boys obviously knew their Hebrew. But this is Peter—a fisherman. This isn't a theologian. This is a guy who caught fish for a living. And he has found the perfect verse to explain the fulfillment of prophecy that is happening.

His sermon isn't exactly roses and buttercups. It's harsh. He tells them the facts in verse 22-24—a man came and did miraculous things…and you killed him. Enter in the big gulp. But Peter isn't finished with his sermon. Because the man they handed over to death could not be killed—he could not be stopped.

---

[58] He finally understands what it means to die to self and live for Christ.

That certainly got their attention! By verse 37, they asked, "Brothers, what shall we do?" (NIV); old Peter probably would have said, "Bend down your necks, that we may cut them off and you can spend all of your days being tortured for your actions." But this is not old Peter—this is the Peter filled with the Spirit. His reply isn't vengeful. It's forgiving, "Repent and be baptized" he tells them in verse 38, "And you will receive the gift of the Holy Spirit." (NIV)

3,000 people became Christians that day according to verse 41. Talk about a powerful sermon! But the details of that number are sketchy at best. 3,000 people would not have fit in that Upper Room. So, what exactly happened? Did Peter go out to a bigger space and preach?

Guesswork is required here. But to begin with, it seems essential to understand that Peter isn't the only Christian here. He may have given the sermon, but there are other ministers present. What is perhaps more believable is that after the Holy Spirit came upon them, a great commotion was caused and people came toward the Upper Room to see what was happening. Think about an accident on the freeway—one accident, thousands of people slowing down to look.

What's probably happened is thousands of people are trying to figure out what all this commotion is about, and the believers leave the Upper Room, and they go tell them. There are 120 in the Upper Room; divide that by 3,000 and you get 25. That means statistically, these 120 people filled with the very Spirit of God only need to find 25 people to tell them about Jesus. If that happens, you get 3,000. That seems like a very believable number.

# # #

Pentecost is an important event. It represents two things for every Christian:

The day a new covenant essentially comes to town and gives birth to Christianity.

The day God reveals himself in the most personal way: The Holy Spirit. It marks the beginning of when all men and women cannot just know of God, but experience God.

The Resurrection was just the event that planted a seed for change for the believers—God spent 50 days growing that seed until it all culminated here. And now it's time for these men and women to go fearlessly to all the world, spreading the Good News.

UNSTOPPABLE CHURCH

The church is only as unstoppable as the Christians inside of it. But churches, no doubt, do play a role in the spread of Christianity. The 1801 Cane Ridge Revival at the Cane Ridge Meeting House is often cited as the birth of the second great awakening.

Cane Ridge is a small town about 20 miles outside of Lexington. Low estimates say 10,000 people attended the meetings; high estimates say 30,000 people. The population of the entire state for Kentucky was about 220,000 at the time. Which means at least 5% of the entire state was at the meeting, but it was probably closer to 10%. Pretty big, right? And remember, this is 1800—cars had not been invented. To get to this event was an all-day affair. And people didn't go home. They camped out. For the 1800s, this was probably the closest thing to the modern-day Coachella Music Festival.

The meetinghouse obviously wouldn't hold all of the people. So, pastors made the best of what they had. There were several stages and several pastors speaking at the same time. It was wild. Pastors standing on tree stumps, covered wagons—whatever they could find.

Part of the success could be attributed to Christians of all backgrounds coming together. This wasn't a Baptist affair. All denominations got involved. Presbyterian, Methodist and Baptist ministers all took turns delivering sermons.

While we don't really know what happened on Pentecost in that Upper Room, it's easy to imagine it looked a little something like this revival—perhaps a little small at first, but then larger and larger until it was spilling out everywhere and Christians were using whatever they could find to preach the Gospel to all who would hear.

EPILOGUE

Something happened.

Something indeed. The disciples had discovered what Jesus Christ had spent his entire ministry getting them ready for. They went from seeing the human side of Christ to the godly side.

Suddenly, the man they followed was more than a man—but it wasn't the Resurrection alone that proved this; throughout the small fragments that exists in each of the Gospels and Acts are small revelations and clues about the divine nature of Christ and his relationship with us. For forty days, Christ taught his disciples what it meant to have a relationship with God; finally, at Pentecost, we see transformed men and women who finally understand what it means to have a personal relationship with God.

Easter is an important day for Christians. It represents an important event. Jesus Christ rose from the dead—he became the sacrificial lamb for our sins.

But next time you celebrate Easter, ask yourself this: what if that was it? What if Easter happened, and Jesus rose from the dead, but there was no Ascension. Jesus went on living—teaching; maybe in forty more years he died of natural causes. What then?

What is Easter—what is Christianity—without the Ascension? It's just a nice story, really. It's the story of Lazarus. A man who rose from the dead. I bet Lazarus led a full life after that—he witnessed to people and said what an amazing thing God had done. And that would have been Jesus. Because the Resurrection is just a miracle when you take the Ascension out of the equation.

If Jesus Christ had merely risen from the dead, then he would be of Earth. Fully man. He didn't Ascend to Heaven because…why not? There was a purpose there. He assumed his role in Heaven for us. Hebrews 9:24 says, "For Christ did not enter a sanctuary made with human hands that was only a copy of the true one; he entered Heaven itself, now to appear for us in God's presence." (NIV) What does this mean? It means Christ didn't conquer the temple on Earth—he didn't assume his place as a priest who was human. He ascended into Heaven—a task a mere human cannot do—and he intercedes for us.

If Jesus Christ had merely resurrected, then we could not have a personal relationship with God. Man would stand on Earth; God would stand in Heaven. But no bridge would connect us to God. Christ is that bridge—his Ascension, not his Resurrection, represented that.

But the Ascension isn't just for us. Ephesians 4:10 says, "He who descended is the very one who ascended higher than all the Heavens, in order to fill the whole universe." (NIV)

Notice the word "universe" there? Is this the makings of something that's out of this world? The Jesus of aliens we don't even know? Perhaps. But more than that, it represents mankind in the most all-encompassing sense. If Jesus had not ascended, then his Resurrection would have been for the age—not the ages. It would have been a great event—a memorable event, indeed—but he would have stayed on Earth. His Ascension represents something out of this world—something with no beginning and no end. Something that doesn't care for the men and women from two thousand years ago, but cares for the people not even born—the people two thousand years in the present—or even two hundred million years in the present. All men. For all time.

For forty days, Jesus was teaching his disciples about this new body—this is new teaching. Prior to the Resurrection, his teachings were about others. But now there's a special emphasis on relationships. On how God dwells in us forever. The disciples began to change when they saw how this worked—when they saw how the Holy Spirit worked—when they saw how it all came together perfectly.

Ephesians 5:30 says, "For we are members of his body, of his flesh, and of his bones." (NIV) That's what he spent forty days teaching. It's about dying to self. Becoming part of Christ. When you no longer live, but Christ lives in you, what does that mean? Suddenly our daily worries no longer exist. We don't wake up in the morning and worry about how we'll pay the bills or how we'll feel happier. We live to show Christ to the world. That's all that matters. Yes, you still have to pay the bills and yes you still have to live in this world, but you do so with the assurance that God will provide. That he will not leave you.

But Ephesians 5:30 is more than that. Because we are "members" of his body. *Members*. That means it's not just you and him. It means we're in this together. We are a community of believers living with one common goal.

The Ascension also represents unity—Christ leaving us to join us together.

Peter may have been the hero at Pentecost—the voice of the body. But the voice is not the most important part of the church. No part is the most important, except the center, which is Christ.

The Gospel didn't spread—Christianity didn't grow—because we had people like Peter or even Paul evangelizing. One man can start a movement, but a group of men can change the world. And so, when Christ ascended into Heaven, he was uniting us. He was making us members of one body.

Christianity was a very small sect of Judaism before the Ascension. Jesus didn't leave the world with a huge following, but he did leave the world with small following who could make his name—his kingdom—huge.

The disciples—the early men—were by no means perfect. We have scandals now and they surely had them then. But when they let the Holy Spirit dwell in them…the things that would happen!

It's easy to believe in the holidays. Christmas. Easter. And everything in between. But the holidays aren't the events that shaped Christianity—that shape us as believers. They get people to come out once or twice a year to sit in a pew and spew out a few festive tunes to make mom happy. But that's not Christianity. Christianity is in the events like the Ascension, which we don't even think about—the events that, when you are open to it, will change your heart and start a revolution inside of you.

# # #

When people think of being a Christian, they often think of people going to church; but Christ didn't return here to tell people about church—in fact, church was never part of Christ's message on Earth. Making disciples was his message. We aren't put on Earth to go to church on Sundays. That's not to say we should use that as an excuse not to go—but that is to say some Christians need to reevaluate their purpose in life.

Luke 14:4 tells the parable of the lost sheep:

> Suppose one of you has a hundred sheep and loses one of them. Doesn't he leave the ninety-nine in the open country and go after the lost sheep until he finds it? (NIV)

The church is fine. It's survived for thousands of years without your help. But there are lost sheep. The Ascension is about finding them.

The disciples realized there was something better—even more miraculous than the Resurrection. They realized that we can have a personal relationship with God, and further that we can give others this relationship. Jesus Christ returned not to show the world a miracle, but to show the world love.

We should think about the church; we should think about the ministries to build people up; we should think about how we can have a better relationship with God. But before we think about any of that, we must remember Christ's command to make disciples—that should be the forefront mission of every Christian.

Not all of us are ministers. Not all of us are even great speakers. But the message of Christianity is simple: God loves us unconditionally—and he forgives us. You don't need to be a minister or great speaker to show that. The 12 disciples that Jesus called to spread his message weren't educated men; most of them weren't the types you'd see at universities or writing books; but they accepted his call and God used them.

Whoever you are and whatever you do, God has called you and he can use you for his purpose. He uses the weak just as he uses the strong. He has given you a command to make disciples.

UNSTOPPABLE CHRISTIANS

There may be a lot of things holding you back—keeping you from being unstoppable. For many, it's age. Your younger years have passed you, so how can God truly use you? It's a fair question. But it's still just an excuse.

Fanny Crosby had age against her. Maybe you've never heard of old Fanny, but you've surely heard a few of her greatest hits; she was a hymnist and wrote such classic church ditties as "Blessed Assurance" and "To God Be the Glory." She wrote over 8,000 hymns and gospels. 8,000. Let that sink in.

That's a lot, right? Now consider the fact that she didn't write her first one until she was over forty. Now consider the fact that she was blind. She also wrote over 1,000 poems, and spoke before Congress to lobby for providing education to the blind.

It's never too late to become unstoppable. Fanny was blind. She was over forty. She had the perfect excuse. Nobody would have blamed her if she stayed home. But she let God use her disability to his glory. She proved what God proves time and time again: he uses the weak to show his strength. He takes everything you're bad at—every reason you have to say, "not me, God"—he takes it and he shows his glory. He shows the unexpected. When someone does something in the name of God that is expected, few people give another look; but when someone does the unexpected in God's name, people tend to give more than a nod their way.

APPENDIX A

THE LEGACY OF THE DISCIPLES

Historically every disciple but John was martyred. There's a chance that two or three other disciples might have also died naturally. But how they died really doesn't matter; what matters, of course, is how they lived.

It's easy to say the disciples were unstoppable Christians, but to really understand how they developed before and after the Ascension, let's take a closer look at each disciple.

Andrew

Andrew wasn't one of the big three of the disciples, but he was certainly one of the key members of the all-star team. Like all the disciples, there are a lot of puzzle pieces that we can put together and begin to see who the disciple "probably" was. We know that Andrew was most likely Peter's brother. In most accounts, he is largely overshadowed by his brother, but his presence is still known and he was no doubt a key member of the early church. The Gospel of John notes that Andrew was a follower of John the Baptist and believed Jesus was the Messiah before his brother.[59]

The fact that Andrew, not Peter, is referenced as a follower of John the Baptist, tells us that he was probably the thinker of the family—while his brother was a hard worker, he was philosophical; it's no wonder that the apostle John, who was of the same temperament, remembers him more fondly than the other gospel accounts.[60]

In the New Testament, Andrew is best known for introducing people to Jesus. In John 1:41, Andrew, upon meeting Jesus, goes to Peter so he can introduce him. In John 6:9, Andrew introduces Jesus to a child who has five barley loaves and two fish. In John 12:20-22, two Greeks wanted an introduction to Jesus; they go to Philip who in turn goes to Andrew, who in turn goes with Philip to Jesus.

By these three accounts, we know something very important about who Andrew was: he found important people and brought them to Christ. He finds Peter who is obviously the Rock that Jesus built his church on; he finds the small child with the loaves who was a key component in the miracle—through him Jesus fed thousands. And he finds the Greeks; these were unclean people; a normal Jew would not have brought them to their teacher—their teacher would want nothing to do with them; but Andrew was able to

[59] John 1:41

[60] John and Andrew probably shared the same passions when it came to studying and reflecting on God's word.

understand—perhaps earlier than the other apostles—that Jesus was blind to races and skin colors—that these unclean people were key to his ministry and would be key to their own ministry.

There are lots of traditions about where Andrew went after the Ascension. We can assume he was very active in his missions work and started several churches.

More important than where he went was who he was. He was second string…but he was okay with that. While his brother was making a name for himself at the top of the pyramid, he was content in telling and bringing people to Christ. Through him, God shows us how he uses instruments—how our legacy is really in the people we bring to Christ—the role we played in the bigger picture. Without Andrew, then Peter would have never come to Christ. Think of all the most influential spiritual leaders in the world—someone introduced them to Christ; but those someones are rarely mentioned and when they are, people don't know who they are. That was Andrew.

It is almost universally accepted that Andrew was martyred. Legends have formed about how and where. The most popular is that he was crucified, but refused to be crucified as Christ was, and requested instead an X-shaped cross, which is now known as St. Andrew's Cross. Many country flags bear the symbol—notably Scotland, where Andrew is the Patron Saint.[61]

---

[61] This after a famous battle when the Scots were outnumbered and the King prayed that if they came out victorious he would name

Bartholomew (Also Known as Nathanael)

Bartholomew was reluctant, to say the least, about Jesus; when Philip ran to him and told him that they had found the one Moses spoke of, he replied: Can anything good come from there (i.e. Nazareth)?[62] Jews in general didn't hold Nazareth in high regard—it was in Galilee, which Matthew 4:15 calls: "Galilee of the Gentiles." This was not the town for good Jewish boys and girls.

Philip didn't argue with Bartholomew and try and explain how indeed something good could come from Nazareth; he told Bartholomew to come and see for himself. And it doesn't take long to completely turn him around. When he meets Jesus, he almost instantly says, "Rabbi you are the Son of God; you are the king of Israel." (John 1:49)

Some of the disciples took a bit longer to recognize who Jesus was. Not Bartholomew. He went out of the gates running! Readers don't see a lot more about Bartholomew, but this verse alone tells us he was on fire for Jesus—it's hard to imagine that flame ever extinguished.

The tradition is that Bartholomew was a missionary in India and Armenia. A church was erected on the site that he is

---

Andrew as the Patron Saint; it is said that an X appeared in the sky on the morning of battle.

[62] John 1:46

believed to have been martyred. How he was martyred is much speculated—theories range from beheaded to skinned alive. The reason for his martyrdom: converting the king of Armenia to Christianity.

James the Elder

James was one of the Brothers of Thunder—named, most likely, for their fiery spirit. He was the brother of the Apostle John—likely his older brother. Some believe that they were Jesus' cousins.

His father owned a successful fishing company and seems to have been a man making a very healthy living. His mom was Salome, who liked to pal around with the Marys and could easily be called an unofficial disciple.

James doesn't play a pivotal role in the gospels, but is a part of the close inner circle of apostles.

Acts 12:2 tells us that James was martyred; this was around 44 AD—approximately ten years after Christ ascended. James was both the first and only apostle that the Bible mentions was martyred. There is no record of why he was martyred—just who did it.[63] Many believe that James had gone to Spain to minister to Jews who had been exiled there,

[63] Herod Agrippa, whose granddad was responsible for murdering babies in Bethlehem.

which did not go over well with Herod, who was the guy who sent them there.

After James, it really was game-on for the church. Up until this moment, they had perhaps been harassed and bullied—but this was an apostle—this was not supposed to happen to the leader of the church. Stephen had, of course, been the first martyr of the church, but his death was likely not as rippling as James'.

Christ had warned Christians that he did not come to bring peace, but the sword;[64] this was not a call to arms, rather a warning that they were now in a time of persecution. That warning was now real, and they had a choice to make: were they willing to die for the cross? James was the first, but not the last, to say yes.

James the Lesser or Younger

James the Lesser seems like an appropriate title because there's hardly anything known about him. Most hold he is the same as James, son of Alphaeus. Some hold that he is the same as James, Brother of Jesus—but this is more debatable. The gospels typically list disciples in order of prominence—three groups: group one is the well-known ones, group two is the ones people know of, and group three are the most obscure

---

[64] Matthew 10:34

ones. That's not to say they weren't important—or that people held them in lesser regard.

We can assume that James was not a leader—he was a follower; he didn't talk back—he listened.

James no doubt played a pivotal role in the growth of Christianity—he just wasn't as vocal as others. Perhaps he played more of a servant role than a leader role?

If you take the position that James the Lesser and James, Brother of Jesus were one in the same, then James became bishop of Jerusalem and was later martyred.

John

John was one of the few apostles who escaped martyrdom—perhaps the only apostle. Most believe John was the youngest apostle. Peter may have been the rock on which Christ built his church, but John was the one who lived to tell the church's story—dying when he was about 92.

It is traditionally accepted that John is the author of the Gospel of John, The Book of Revelations, and the First Epistle of John (many believe the other Epistles bearing his name were written by another John).

The stories he must have had to tell—he had seen all of his brothers and sisters in Christ die—suffering for what they believed. Unlike any other Christian in history, he was able to look back and see what had become of it—how it had grown and spread. Unlike the other gospels, which were written much earlier to convert believers, John's gospel seems to be an attempt to mature Christians—he's writing to make sure what really happened is documented. There were already people making up things about the church, and he wanted to make sure people knew the real story.

John was the philosopher of the group, and to him was tasked one of Christianity's greatest responsibilities: write the final book of the New Testament—the prophecy of what is to come.

It's likely that after his brother, James, suffered martyrdom, the apostles realized that they could no longer be close; if the church was to survive, then the disciples would have to scatter.

It is traditionally held that John wrote the Book of Revelations while in exile. According to this tradition, he was first put into boiling oil, but he did not die—he was not even burned.

Judas Iscariot

Judas committed suicide. Sunday school teaches us that much. So do pastors. Today we really don't think much about him. He's the guy who betrayed Jesus and killed himself.

But people thought differently thousands of years ago. While most certainly saw him as the betrayer, there are lots of stories about him.

The Gospel of Judas,[65] for example, tells an account of Jesus instructing Judas to betray him; Judas' action, therefore, was not an act of betrayal, rather of obedience. Judas, further, was given teachings the other disciples had not received.

If you believe in secret teachings, you might be a Gnostic, because that is essentially what's going on in the book. The book is dated, at the earliest, 120 AD, which means it came about much too late to being taken seriously as a canonical work—still, it shows us that *some* people did believed much differently about Judas than we do today.

In *The Gospel of Barnabas*,[66] Judas is transformed into the image of Jesus and takes his place at the crucifixion. How did Jesus rise from the dead? He didn't, according to this account, he never actually died—Judas did.

You can take the Sunday school version of Judas and say he's the guy responsible for Jesus' death, but if you believe that Jesus forgives all sins, then what about betrayal? In Matthew 26:50, Jesus calls Judas "friend" even when he knows what he's doing—he seems willing to forgive even in Judas' darkest moment. It should also be noted, however, that Judas never called Jesus Lord—he always referred to him as a Rabbi.

---

[65] An Apocryphal work written in the second century.

[66] Dated even further than the Gospel of Judas—most give it a date in the 15th century at the earliest.

Was Judas forgiven? It certainly was a question on the mind of the early church. The answer really depends on whether he had finally concluded that Jesus was Lord. The Bible is clear that suicide is sin, but it's not the worst thing you can do—the worst thing is dying without realizing who Jesus really is.

Jude or Thaddeus

Just as Hitler pretty much killed the toothbrush mustache, Judas Iscariot sort of killed the name Judas; so much so that even the people in the Bible didn't want to include the name for fear people would associate it with *that* Judas. Case in point: that other apostle, Judas. Matthew and Mark call him Thaddeus; John calls him Judas not Iscariot; and Luke calls him Jude. Jude is what people know him as today.

Jude may or may not have written the Epistle of Jude; he also may or may not have been the brother of Jesus. He could have also been a cousin.

He may or may not have been vegetarians' best friend, because many traditions say he didn't eat meat. Jude the vegetarian stems from a work by Hegesippus,[67] who said that Jude did not drink alcohol or eat meat. Don't go running to your local library to dig up Hegesippus—his work is almost

[67] A first century chronicler of Christianity.

entirely lost, with the exception of a few quotes that Eusebius[68] uses.[69]

Jude is best known to Christians as the guy who asked a question. In John 14:22, he says during the Last Supper, "But, Lord, why do you intend to show yourself to us and not to the world?" (NIV)

According to tradition, Jude was martyred with Simon the Zealot.

Matthew or Levi

Matthew was originally a tax collector before Jesus called him to follow him. Traditionally, Matthew wrote the Gospel of Matthew, but the Gospel itself never makes reference to who the author is (or isn't) and the title "Gospel of Matthew" was not applied to it until years afterward. He may have written it; or he may not have.

There are elements of the Gospel that point to his authorship—the fact that it's written for a Jewish audience, for instance; also of note is the fact that three fifths of the Gospel

---

[68] Another early church historian.

[69] And in case you're wondering, Jewish vegetarianism is actually a thing; it stems from the belief that the Torah implies Jews should maintain a meatless diet. And for the record, while the Torah does not directly forbid eating meat (except pork), it also does not say it's required.

is actual things that Jesus said—whoever wrote it had to have been there to record it.

Because of his status as a tax collector, we can assume that he had a significant amount of money, and before his call, all of the apostles either knew him or knew of him.

Traditionally, he died a martyr, but this has never been proven.

Peter or Simon Peter

Peter is the rock. The leader of the early Christian church—even the first Pope, if you are a Catholic. It is generally accepted that Peter wrote the first epistle of Peter, but the second is more debatable. Because the Gospel of Mark seems to have a Peter tone to it, it was originally thought to have been written by Peter's traveling companion, Mark; today, most scholars accept that there's no way to know who wrote the Gospel.

During Pentecost, it's Peter who gives the first sermon in all Christianity. Peter is fierier than ever, and it's clear who's going to lead the early movement of believers.

As passionate as Peter was to lead the church, he was slower to change it. He wasn't quite happy at first with how Gentiles should be treated; and he wasn't as far traveled as some of the other apostles. He's mostly seen managing the church.

Peter was martyred. Traditionally in Rome, but that most likely was not the case. Most believe it was ordered by Nero after the great fire of 64.[70] Some legends say upside down, but this is most likely not true.

Philip

There are two notable Philips in the Bible. Philip the Evangelist and Philip the Apostle. People often mistake the two as being the same person. Philip the Evangelist appears in the sixth and eighth chapter of the Acts of the Apostles—but he's not the same as the disciple.

If you always thought Philip the Apostle and Philip the Evangelist were one in the same, then you are not alone; many of the early church fathers felt the same way, which led to many apocryphal accounts that were simply false (Eusebius, one of the most noted early Christian fathers, was one of the people who got the two confused). How do we know they aren't the same? The Bible tells us so. In Acts 6, the 12 disciples got together to pick seven deacons, and it lists this second Philip as one of the seven.

What do we know about Philip the Apostle? Not a lot.

---

[70] Nero blamed Christians for that fire—some say it was actually Nero who started the fire, but that is debatable.

We know that Philip isn't a Hebrew name, but he was Hebrew; that tells us that while his parents were Jewish, they were a little more liberal because they didn't pick a Jewish name.

John 1:44, tells us that he was from the city of Bethsaida, but John also notes that his was the town of Andrew and Peter—a note that has made some speculate that John is implying they were friends before Jesus. If that's the case, then Andrew, who, prior to becoming one of Jesus' disciples was a disciple of John the Baptist, probably had lots of long discussions with Philip about John's ministry.

Philip wasn't quick to come to a decision—in fact, Philip didn't find Jesus; Jesus found Philip. John 1:43 says, "The next day Jesus decided to leave for Galilee. Finding Philip, he said to him, 'Follow me.' (NIV) What's curious is Philip then goes to Nathanael in verse 45 and says, "We have found the one Moses wrote about in the law." (NIV) That seems like a mighty bold move on Philip's part since he didn't exactly find Jesus—but that's not what Philip is saying; he's not saying he went out seeking to find the Messiah and he did just that. He's saying he was empty, but he found the void to make him whole.

The fact that Philip is referencing Moses and the Old Testament tells us that he is a good Jewish boy who has no doubt heard about the coming Messiah; every Jew during this period was looking for the Messiah.

What else does the Bible tell us about Philip? It tells us more about his character—who he was as a person—than what he actually did.

John 6:1-15 shows Jesus preaching to a huge crowd—thousands of people; Jesus went to Philip and basically said, "Hey, we need to feed these people—they're hungry." Philip is puzzled—he has no idea how to do that, and tells Jesus it would take half a year's wage to buy enough bread for each person to have a single bite. It doesn't say what Jesus said to Philip—perhaps he didn't have time to say anything at all, because Andrew speaks up and tells Jesus about a boy with bread and fish.

John 12:21 shows two Gentiles asking Philip to get them an invitation to see Jesus; Philip in turn goes to Andrew, who goes with Philip to ask Jesus about it. That's not very exciting. Except it tells us two important things. First, it shows that Philip doesn't quite know what to do about Gentiles; and second, it shows his relationship with Andrew. Why can't Philip go alone to see Jesus about this Gentile question he has? The fact that John has mentioned Philip twice and both times Andrew is also mentioned tells us that the two were probably pretty close.

In John 14, we see Philip one final time; in the Upper Room before his crucifixion, Philip challenges Jesus; Jesus tells his disciples in 14:6-7 that he is "the way and the truth and the life. No one comes to the Father except through me. If you really know me, you will know my Father as well. From now on, you do know him and you have seen him." (NIV) He's telling his disciples that he is God! It's a divine moment! And then Philip speaks up…

He tells Jesus in verse 8 that if he shows them the Father, then that will be enough.

What Jesus says in reply to this is basically an epic, "Are you kidding me, Philip?!" For the next several verses, Jesus reiterates who the Father is.

Some of the disciples are bold. Some are rather quiet. And some are simply ordinary. Philip was of the ordinary variety. There really was nothing special about him. He wasn't bold—and when he is bold, it's about something he shouldn't be bold about. But God took this ordinary man and he used him to his glory.

After the Ascension, non-Biblical tradition says that he became a missionary in what is now the country of Turkey—not too far from Ephesus, where the Apostle John eventually settled.

And again, going off tradition, Philip performed a miracle in what is now the country of Turkey on the wife of a high-ranking city official; through the miracle and his teaching he converted her. This didn't go over well with her husband, who ordered Philip and Bartholomew to be crucified upside-down. Bartholomew was eventually released, but Philip supposedly asked that he himself be left on the cross. Was he martyred? Probably. Was he martyred in this way? Probably not. There were other traditions about what happened, but they conflict. There are enough traditions to make it easy to speculate that he indeed was killed. It's just hard to say how. In 2011, archaeologists uncovered a tomb that some believe belongs to Philip. The tomb is in Turkey in the region he is believed to have been martyred.

Simon the Zealot

Simon the Zealot is the most obscure of all the apostles. He was an apostle—that much the Bible tells us. But that's about all we know.

We also know he was a Zealot. A Zealot? Not familiar with the group? They were basically the Jewish mafia. You didn't want to mess around with them. The group started as a way of getting the Roman Empire out of the Holy Land. The Jews had been ridiculously taxed.[71] These weren't the Bernie Sanders kind of fanatics who waved their hands in the air and rallied people up but were ultimately peaceful; these were the stabby kind of fanatics—the kind that would stab anyone they thought to be a traitor.

So, Simon was a knife-carrying member of his local Zealot club? Possibly, but probably not. Not all Zealots were as radical as others. The main component of all Zealots was they wanted Rome out of their land.

When you look at all the disciples, you begin to see that they each had unique characteristics that made them a diverse—yet perfect—bunch. You had the leaders, the philosophers, and the caregivers. And you have Simon the Zealot—a man willing to carry his passions to the extreme. The Zealots were a violent bunch of revolutionaries; the disciples were peace-loving group of revolutionaries—the contrast here is

---

[71] Some say up to 40% of their income went to taxes—and no, they weren't able to write off their lambs as a tax deduction.

hard to miss. One cannot say with certainty why Jesus picked the disciples he picked, but one cannot help but see how he turned a man who must have been full of fiery rage into a man who was full of fiery love.

There are lots of stories of what happened to Simon the Zealot—some say he traveled as far as England; most believe he was martyred—murdered, no doubt, by the souls full of the same rage he used to have.

Thomas

Thomas doubted. That's what the Bible tells us. That's what he's remembered for. And that's a shame because Thomas did so much more than doubt—realistically, that's the least he should be remembered for. But Thomas probably wouldn't mind much, because it was as a result of that doubt that he accomplished so much. He lived the rest of his days doubting no more.

Some believe that Thomas was the twin brother of Matthew; his name, Thomas, means twin, so it's easy to believe that he was the twin of someone. Some also believe that Matthew was the prodigal son in the parable that Jesus tells; if that's true, then Thomas was the brother who stayed home—who was cautious, which fits his personality.

Thomas is remembered by Catholics as being present at the assumption of Mary—a doctrine Protestants do not traditionally accept—where, according to legends, Thomas was in India when he was transported to her tomb to witness her assumption into Heaven.

It's widely accepted that Thomas was a missionary in India until his death; in fact, he traveled perhaps more than any other disciple.

Some of the earliest apocryphal writings have born Thomas' name;[72] while the writings are too late to be included in the Bible,[73] they do tell us how interested people were in the life of this doubter.

Most believe that Thomas died as a Martyr in India.

Matthias 12th Disciple After Judas Betrayed

Matthias is an easy apostle to forget. He's mentioned in Acts 1:23-26 and then is essentially forgotten—but not gone. While the Bible is void of Matthias, he had a very active ministry.

We know that Matthias, while not an original disciple, was with Jesus during his ministry; it was one of the requirements

---

[72] Including the Infancy Gospel of Thomas about the boyhood of Jesus; the Gospel of Thomas, which consist of sayings of Jesus; and the Acts of Thomas, which is largely about his missions after the Ascension.

[73] The dating is about 100 to 300 AD.

for being chosen—he had to be an eyewitness of Jesus and see the Resurrection. This is what we know with absolute certainty. From here, we have to start leaning a lot on tradition.

Tradition tells us that he did a lot of church planting in what is now Turkey and Georgia. Again, according to tradition, he was stoned to death in Georgia. There is a marker for his grave in Georgia, but that does not necessarily mean that's where he's buried—there are lots of claims about where disciples were buried. There are also claims that he was stoned in Jerusalem as well as what is now Turkey.

About the only thing anyone seems to agree with is that he died a martyr.

UNSTOPPABLE CHRISTIANS

The disciples were sort of the all-star team. In 1885, there was another sort of all-star team making waves around the country: The Cambridge Seven.

The Cambridge Seven was composed of six Cambridge students and one from the Royal Military Academy. These were men who came from well-to-do families; men who knew that a life of comfort awaited them after college. But comfort didn't quite suit them.

At the time, Hudson Taylor was making waves of his own by opening up China to missionaries. Christianity had been in China prior to Taylor, and there were certainly other missionaries in China; but Taylor is most commonly cited for opening the floodgates. Through his mission,[74] over 800 missionaries came to the country and opened over 125 schools. Taylor didn't just come to the country as some missionaries did—he immersed himself in the country by wearing their clothes, learning their culture and speaking their language.

The Cambridge Seven heard Taylor and accepted his call to be missionaries in China.

They were paraded around England and used as examples of how God can turn anyone into a missionary. Men who believed God didn't want them to be comfortable…he wanted them to be unstoppable.

While not all seven stayed in China for their entire lives, all seven remained in ministry.

---

[74] China Inland Mission.

APPENDIX B

REFERENCE TO THE ASCENSION

Psalm 47:5 - God has ascended amid shouts of joy, the LORD amid the sounding of trumpets. (NIV)

Psalm 68:18 - When you ascended on high, you took many captives; you received gifts from people, even from the rebellious—that you, LORD God, might dwell there. (NIV)

Mark 16:19 - After the Lord Jesus had spoken to them, he was taken up into heaven and he sat at the right hand of God. (NIV)

Luke 24:26 - Did not the Messiah have to suffer these things and then enter his glory? (NIV)

Luke 24:50-51 - When he had led them out to the vicinity of Bethany, he lifted up his hands and blessed them. 51 While he was blessing them, he left them and was taken up into heaven. (NIV)

John 1:51 - He then added, "Very truly I tell you, you will see 'heaven open, and the angels of God ascending and descending on' the Son of Man." (NIV)

John 6:62 - Then what if you see the Son of Man ascend to where he was before! (NIV)

John 7:33-34 - Jesus said, "I am with you for only a short time, and then I am going to the one who sent me. 34 You will look for me, but you will not find me; and where I am, you cannot come." (NIV)

John 7:39 - By this he meant the Spirit, whom those who believed in him were later to receive. Up to that time the Spirit had not been given, since Jesus had not yet been glorified. (NIV)

John 14:2-4 - My Father's house has many rooms; if that were not so, would I have told you that I am going there to prepare a place for you? 3 And if I go and prepare a place for you, I will come back and take you to be with me that you also may be where I am. 4 You know the way to the place where I am going." (NIV)

John 14:12 - Very truly I tell you, whoever believes in me will do the works I have been doing, and they will do even greater things than these, because I am going to the Father. (NIV)

John 14:28 - "You heard me say, 'I am going away and I am coming back to you.' If you loved me, you would be glad that I am going to the Father, for the Father is greater than I. (NIV)

John 16:5 - but now I am going to him who sent me. None of you asks me, 'Where are you going?' (NIV)

John 16:7 - But very truly I tell you, it is for your good that I am going away. Unless I go away, the Advocate will not come to you; but if I go, I will send him to you. (NIV)

John 16:10 - about righteousness, because I am going to the Father, where you can see me no longer; (NIV)
John 16:16 - Jesus went on to say, "In a little while you will see me no more, and then after a little while you will see me." (NIV)
John 16:25 - "Though I have been speaking figuratively, a time is coming when I will no longer use this kind of language but will tell you plainly about my Father. (NIV)
John 16:28 - I came from the Father and entered the world; now I am leaving the world and going back to the Father." (NIV)
John 17:5 - And now, Father, glorify me in your presence with the glory I had with you before the world began. (NIV)
John 17:13 - "I am coming to you now, but I say these things while I am still in the world, so that they may have the full measure of my joy within them. (NIV)
John 20:17 - Jesus said, "Do not hold on to me, for I have not yet ascended to the Father. Go instead to my brothers and tell them, 'I am ascending to my Father and your Father, to my God and your God.'" (NIV)
Acts 1:9 - After he said this, he was taken up before their very eyes, and a cloud hid him from their sight. (NIV)
Acts 3:21 - Heaven must receive him until the time comes for God to restore everything, as he promised long ago through his holy prophets. (NIV)
Romans 8:34 - Who then is the one who condemns? No one. Christ Jesus who died—more than that, who was raised to life—is at the right hand of God and is also interceding for us. (NIV)

Ephesians 1:20 - he exerted when he raised Christ from the dead and seated him at his right hand in the heavenly realms, (NIV)

Ephesians 4:8-10 - This is why it says: “When he ascended on high, he took many captives and gave gifts to his people.” 9 (What does “he ascended” mean except that he also descended to the lower, earthly regions? 10 He who descended is the very one who ascended higher than all the heavens, in order to fill the whole universe.) (NIV)

Philippians 2:9-11 - Therefore God exalted him to the highest place and gave him the name that is above every name, 10 that at the name of Jesus every knee should bow, in heaven and on earth and under the earth, 11 and every tongue acknowledge that Jesus Christ is Lord, to the glory of God the Father. (NIV)

1 Timothy 3:16 Beyond all question, the mystery from which true godliness springs is great: He appeared in the flesh, was vindicated by the Spirit, was seen by angels, was preached among the nations, was believed on in the world, was taken up in glory. (NIV)

Hebrews 1:3 - The Son is the radiance of God’s glory and the exact representation of his being, sustaining all things by his powerful word. After he had provided purification for sins, he sat down at the right hand of the Majesty in heaven. (NIV)

Hebrews 4:14 - Therefore, since we have a great high priest who has ascended into heaven, Jesus the Son of God, let us hold firmly to the faith we profess. (NIV)

Jesus Ascended. What Does That Mean?

Hebrews 9:24 - For Christ did not enter a sanctuary made with human hands that was only a copy of the true one; he entered heaven itself, now to appear for us in God's presence. (NIV)

1 Peter 3:22 - who has gone into heaven and is at God's right hand—with angels, authorities and powers in submission to him. (NIV)

TIMELINE OF EVENTS

- Jesus appears to Mary Magdalene (Mark 16:9-11, John 20:11-18)
- Jesus appears to Mary, Salome, Joanna (Matthew 28:1, Mark 16:1, Luke 24:10)
- Jesus appears to Peter (Luke 24:34)
- Jesus appears to Cleopas and his companion (Luke 24:13-35)
- Jesus appears to the disciples (minus Thomas) (Luke 24:36-43, John 20:19-25)
- Jesus appears to disciples (including Thomas) (John 20:26-29)
- Seven of the disciples at the Sea of Tiberius (John 21:1-23)
- Disciples and a large gathering at Galilee (Matthew 28:16-17)
- The Ascension (Luke 24:50-52)
- Pentecost (Acts 2:1-40)

Jesus Ascended. What Does That Mean?

DISCUSSION QUESTIONS

Prologue

1. What was Easter like for you as a child? Share a few memories.
2. Have you ever thought about the Ascension? What does it mean to you?
3. Do you think the Ascension is essential to Christian faith? If it didn't happen, would it matter?
4. Each Gospel has a different message and audience. Which one speaks to you the most and why?
5. Have you ever met a Christian who seems to have unstoppable faith? What stands out about them?

Chapter 1

1. Can you remember the first time you heard the Resurrection story? If not, share when the story became more significant for you?

2. When Jesus rises, nobody actually sees it; he just starts appearing to people. It's very subtle. Why do you think this is?
3. Why do you think Jesus appeared to the women before anyone else?
4. Do you think it's unusual that the women do not recognize Jesus? Do you think he looked different, or do you think the women are just in shock?
5. If Jesus appeared to you, what's the first thing you would do? Who would you tell? Would it change the way you believe, or make you more devoted?

Chapter 2

1. Have you ever had a mysterious encounter or a time where you felt a divine intervention?
2. Jesus gave a Bible study to the two men; if Jesus walked into your Bible study and could give a lesson on any book or topic in the Bible, what would you want it to be?
3. Jesus scolded these men for their weak belief; do you think Jesus would scold you?
4. Why do you think these men were "kept" from recognizing Jesus?
5. What does it mean to walk by faith not by sight?

Chapter 3

1. There's a meeting with Peter that is never explained in the Bible—except to say it happened—what do you think happened?
2. When the women tell the disciples about what happened, Peter and John take off running. If someone told you that Jesus had appeared at a specific location, how would you approach it? Would you run? Walk? Wait and see what others think? See if Fox News covers the story?
3. Why do you think the disciples are so afraid when Jesus returns?
4. The disciples think Jesus is a ghost at first; why can't Jesus be a ghost? Do you think ghosts are real? If so, what role do you think they play?
5. What does it mean to "receive the Holy Spirit"?

Chapter 4

1. Share a time when you felt you missed out on something.
2. Put yourself in Thomas' shoes; all your friends have seen Jesus and you have not. How would you feel? Would you believe your friends? Or would you be skeptical?

3. If you go to church, do you feel comfortable or challenged? If you don't go to church, what keeps you away?
4. The Bible doesn't say what happened after Thomas believed. What do you think happened? Do you think Jesus simply left? Do you think there was a teaching?
5. Do you believe stigmata is a real thing?

Chapter 5

1. Is there a place you like to escape to? A home away from home?
2. Do you think it's odd that after Jesus appeared to the disciples, they go back to work? Would life go on as usual for you?
3. Picture yourself in the boat with the disciples; Jesus appears on the shore. Who would you be? Would you be like Peter jumping into the water so you can get there quicker? Would you stay in the boat? Would you row the other way because you're terrified of what Jesus would say to you?
4. Why do you think Jesus let them catch so many fish—especially when he'd already prepared a meal for them?
5. What do you think is the significance of Jesus asking Peter three times if he loves him?

Chapter 6

1. Have you ever gone on a mission trip? If so, share where you went and what the trip meant to you. Did you grow at all? If you haven't, is there anything that holds you back or is it something you would like to do one day?
2. Jesus has now appeared to all of them and yet during the Great Commission, it says that some of them still doubted. How is that even possible? What do you think their thought process is?
3. Jesus rebukes them for doubting; we often hear about the loving side of Jesus, but not so much the rebuking side—does it surprise you when you hear about this side of Jesus? Is there anything in your life that you think he'd be disappointed by?
4. What does baptism mean to you? When were you baptized and what did it mean to you? If you haven't been baptized, is there anything that holds you back from it?
5. Is there anyone or any group that you feel called to share the Gospel with, but you are afraid to?

Chapter 7

1. Have you ever heard a really weird non-Biblical story about Jesus?

2. Even if apocryphal works aren't true, do you think we should study them?
3. Does anything surprise you about the apocryphal works the author mentions?
4. Do you think Mary was a virgin for life? Do you think this is an important teaching? Why or why not?
5. Do you think Jesus appearing to 500 and 120 is the same thing? If not, what do you think happened when he appeared to 500, and why isn't it recorded in more detail?

Chapter 8

1. If you knew you were going to die, what would your last words be?
2. What do you think the Ascension looked like?
3. Do you think the Ascension was something that spiritually happened or physically happened?
4. What does it mean to you when it says in Ephesians 4:8 that Christ led "captivity captive"?
5. What does worship mean to you?

Chapter 9

1. What's something in your life that you feel you were unprepared for—that you were just kind of tossed into? How did you get through it?

2. Why do you think Jesus Ascended after forty days? Why not 3? Why not 300? What's so special about forty?
3. Why is Pentecost so important? And why is there not the same emphasis placed on it as Easter or Christmas?
4. What does it mean to you to be filled with the Holy Spirit?
5. Do you think people can still speak in tongues today? Why or why not?

Chapter 10

1. What disciple do you relate to?
2. Did any of the post-Resurrection lives of the disciples jump out at you or surprise you?
3. If you were a disciple, do you think you would be in Jesus' inner circle?
4. Do you think you could die for your faith? If so, do you think it makes you weak in faith if you can't die for it or are afraid to die for it?
5. Do you think Judas was forgiven?

Epilogue

Jesus Ascended. What Does That Mean?

1. Would Christianity change for you if Christ had simply risen from the dead, lived out his days, and died of natural causes?
2. What does it mean to be members of Christ's body?
3. What does Christ's command to make disciples mean to you?
4. What spiritual gifts do you have?
5. What would you look like as an unstoppable Christian?

PART TWO: BETHLEHEM, THE YEAR JESUS WAS BORN

Bethlehem, the Year Jesus Was Born

UNWRAPPING THE THEOLOGY BEHIND CHRISTMAS

ORGANIC FAITH SERIES
BOOK TWO

SCOTT DOUGLAS

For Diana, who helped me love Christmas all over again

INTRODUCTION

I am ten. The year is 1988. For days, I have been looking at the giant box under the Christmas tree. Attached to it is a small tag:

From Santa; To Cookie

Cookie is our sometimes loyal, but forever loved, beagle.

My brother and I have been discussing the box from the moment we saw it under the tree more than a week prior. What could it be? Why had Santa brought our dog something? And why had he brought it early?

Cookie, of course, takes no interest in the large package when Christmas morning finally comes—she is too involved in the giant bone my parents had given her that morning—so my brother and I help her with the package. We open it with the wild enthusiasm and madness that every kid has on Christmas morning. And seconds later, the present to Cookie is revealed:

A Nintendo gaming system bundled with a Power Pad and the game *World Class Track Meet*.

My parents had learned a lesson from Christmas' past and disguised the gift so we would not be able to guess what it was.

I'm going to take a wild guess here: you probably have a memory of your very own about a gift you received one Christmas.

Maybe it was something someone made you. Maybe the most meaningful gift was no gift at all. Or maybe the gift you remember most is an NES with Power Pad. Whatever it is, we all have some memory—good or bad—to unwrap.

Every Christian knows the real meaning of Christmas, but when push comes to shove, even if we don't want to admit it, gifts are what Christmas has come to represent for most of us.

Don't worry! This isn't a book to make you realize how vain we all are—how we should forget those gifts and make Christmas about Jesus. I'm not going to guilt-trip you into giving to charities instead of that person who has way too many things or spending Christmas at a homeless shelter instead of drinking hot cocoa next to the fireplace. If that's something God is calling you to do, then you don't need a book to get you there.

So cast aside your worries, because I'll be the first to say: there's nothing wrong with giving and receiving gifts on Christmas.

This book is to help us dissect what Christmas *really* is. Yes, most of us know the story—even people who don't believe the story know the story. But the fact is, thousands of years of history have made the story a little—one dimensional.

Christmas is about gifts. It's about that Nativity story. The Wise Men and their gifts. But why? Why do we give gifts? What is the significance of Jesus being born in a nativity? Or that the Wise Men gave the gifts that they gave?

If you are the person who starts Christmas decorating in the summer, I'm not about to shatter your dreams. I love Christmas—and not just the historical Christmas.

And if you're the Christmas pageant director, don't worry, you can still have that play.

But there's more to Christmas than a staged hour play can teach us; there's more to Christmas than coming around the dinner table or sitting around the Christmas tree and opening gifts. There's more to Christmas than even a savior being born.

The Bible teaches us the real story of Christmas. The problem is people have taken this story and added on to it. Cultures have added on to it. It's passed through countries, and they've tacked on their little spin.

We have thousands of years of a Christmas that is built around legends and myths. The Christmas we know is, in places, more a fairytale. It's an inspiring one for sure. But a fairytale, nonetheless.

When you begin to unwrap the many layers of the first Christmas, you begin to see that there's more to Christmas than meets the eye. God is giving us a message—a gift to unwrap. It's time to slow down and unpack the layers so we can see just how beautiful this gift really is.

After all, would it really have mattered if Mary had given birth in her sister's living room as opposed to a manger? Or if

Jesus was born in Rome instead of Bethlehem? Or what if one of the Wise Men gave Jesus a donkey as a gift instead of frankincense?

I want to keep all of those Christmas memories from childhood…but I also know that there's more to it than gifts—than church nativity pageants—and Christmas lights. There are so many layers to Christmas that most believers never really unpack it. There are details that have been forgotten—details that actually mean something.

This is the story of Christmas. Christmas: God's gift to us.

ONE

THE INCARNA-WHAT NOW?

If you want to learn about Christmas, you'd think that the obvious place to point your eyes would be the Bible. You'll certainly find some of the stories you know there, but Christmas is something you will have a hard time finding in two of the gospels: Mark and John—two writers who didn't mention Jesus' birth at all.

Isn't that mighty curious? Mark is believed to be the first gospel written; and John is believed to be the last. And neither of them thought people would want to know about this miraculous birth?

Let's sit and pause for a moment. Think for a second about all the people in your life who were implanted with the seed of God as a virgin. Aside from that creepy guy in front of the Walmart who keeps trying to get you to join his cult, I'm going to go out on a limb here and say you probably can't think of anyone.

Virgin birth is kind of miraculous. Don't you think it's a story people would want to hear? Sure, John might be able to get away with, "We've all read the story! I was trying to write what people didn't already know." It's not the best excuse, but it makes sense. But what about Mark? He had the honor of telling the story of Jesus before anyone else, and he thought this was one detail that should be missed?

Theologians have argued for years about the reason. The most logical is the audience the gospel writers were writing for would not have found it the most interesting thing about Jesus' life. Mark's gospel is very punchy. It's the shortest book because he's trying to get out the most important details as quickly as possible. The audience was Roman, and Jesus' Jewish genealogy would not have mattered a lot to them. John, contrary to Mark, was writing something highly philosophical.

John 20:30 says, "Jesus performed many other signs in the presence of his disciples, which are not recorded in this book." (NIV) This tells us that there definitely are miracles like the virgin birth that are not in his book; further, there are probably miracles not in any gospel. There are probably dozens of DVDs out there full of deleted scenes from the Bible—hundreds—maybe thousands—of miracles that didn't make the cut. Ultimately, people came to Jesus for the miracles, but they believed in Jesus because of the message—because of what he stood for; so the authors knew they couldn't just fill the pages with miracle after miracle—they had to spend time explaining the miracles so people would believe.

So now, as we finally arrive at the theme of this chapter—the incarnation—it's important to realize that these stories aren't in the Bible because they're good stories to tell.

They're there for a reason. They're there because of all the dozens and dozens of stories the authors could have picked—but they picked this one.

This makes us ask the question, why. Why did Matthew and Luke add it? I'm sure you'll agree that the idea that Jesus was born from a virgin is quite fascinating…but, does it matter? Could it be that this is just a story? And if it was, would that matter? Would our faith be crushed without it?

There's actually a scientific term for this kind of conception: parthenogenesis. Komodo dragons are a good example of things that can produce offspring with or without sex. Thanks to science treating experiments with complete ethical disregard, there is an entire shady study of trying to create babies like this—the goal being to create a species with no illness or genetic irregularities.[75]

If Mary *really* did give birth to Jesus as a virgin, does that really make him holy? Even the apocryphal Jewish book of 2 Enoch has a person (Melchizedek) being virgin-born. So there could be precedence for virgins giving birth to children.

To really understand virgin birth, you have to first understand the doctrine of incarnation.

It's easy to take a very watered-down approach to the incarnation. At its core, it means that Jesus is fully human and fully God. He came from man; he came from God. It's also easy to say that God did this so that we know he existed. This is only part of it.

[75] In other words, the perfect human—at least by scientific standards.

The theology behind the doctrine of incarnation was something early Christians struggled with—it was perhaps easier for some, like gentiles, to accept that a man could be both man and God, than a Jewish believer who had been raised with a very strict and ritualistic belief in God that was pretty void of any personal nature.

Christians did not have a definition of incarnation until the First Council of Nicaea (325), and a concrete definition until the Council of Chalcedon (451). That's a lot of time between, isn't it? And even as it took shape in the church, there continued to be a debate about its foundation.[76]

So what is the non-watered-down version of the incarnation? It's composed of three things:

1. Jesus Christ is divine.
2. Jesus Christ is human.
3. There is union—Jesus Christ is both human and God—two natures in one person.

But this is still a little watered-down because it shows us the what, but not the why. Why did he have to become this incarnate being in the first place? Why not send a prophet or some other messenger? Or why couldn't he come in fully God form?

God didn't have to come to Earth to let us know he existed. Faith is something that exists without proof. God came to Earth to show us that he is close to us.

[76] I'm looking at you, Michael Servetus.

I realize I said John doesn't mention Jesus' birth story. That's only kind of true. John 1:14 says the "Word became flesh." That's the incarnation in a nutshell—that's Jesus' origin story in a nutshell. It's God coming out of the Bible—coming out of the word that we knew about him—and coming to us in human form so we can know him at a personal level. It's God saying, "you don't have to settle for understanding me—you can meet me and know me personally."

God became a human so he could show us that he truly suffered for us—that he understood the pain that we felt.

So when we start thinking about the virgin birth in terms of this doctrine of incarnation, we begin to see that the Bible doesn't make sense without the virgin birth. Virgin birth isn't part of some legend. If we take it out of the equation, suddenly, the theology we hold to be true does not hold up.

Christmas begins at the incarnation—that moment in time when God came and said there would no longer be separation between him and us.

Matthew was writing to an audience who certainly knew about this separation; and Luke was trying to compose the most historically accurate portrayal of Jesus' life. Both understood that their readers, in particular, needed to know what the birth of Jesus really meant.

TWO

HAPPY BIRTHDAY, JESUS?

Before we dive in deep and start really examining the Christmas story, we are going to take a detour and think for a moment about the actual holiday. Appendix C will look even deeper at some of the Christmas traditions over the ages, but the one I'm speaking of here is the actual date of Christmas.

I don't think I'm going to crush any spirits by saying that Christmas is very likely not Jesus' birthday. Most people know this. If you didn't know this, then I'm sorry to be the bearer of bad news, but if Jesus walks into IHOP on Christmas morning, he's not going to get his free birthday breakfast.

Christmas is obviously when we celebrate his birthday, but the actual date is debatable.

Does that matter? Is there a teaching lesson even in the date?

The date is not exactly Biblical, so from a hermeneutics standpoint, there are no real lessons to be drawn here; but the date does have an interesting history that's worth dwelling on before we get to what the Bible *actually* says about Christmas.

JESUS' BIRTHDAY?

I can remember the first time someone told me that Jesus wasn't born on Christmas; I don't remember the date exactly, but I remember it was around Christmas and it was a kid using this rationale as a way to disprove Christ existed.

I didn't follow the logic exactly, but it went along the lines of if people "lied" about this, then they lied about everything else.

It was a silly theory, I realize now. It basically says that because man created something God had no part of, then Christ never existed.

Silly as it is, it's still worth asking, why do we celebrate Jesus' birthday on Christmas? We don't know Jesus' birthday. It's not in the Bible. It's not recorded anywhere. And we are left with only remotely educated guesses. Why not make it summer? Or heck, January 1, so we can get a two for one deal on parties.

While we don't know Jesus' *real* birthday, we do know the date was chosen around 400 AD. Pope Julius is who decided it would be December 25. And yes, there were some pagan holidays around this time, but picking the date wasn't entirely about conversions. It was more about culture. It was the church's way of saying, "Hey, you already got this thing you are celebrating. We don't want to take away the celebrating part, so we're just going to call it something else."

Not long after, around 480 AD, Christians began using the word "Advent"—which was Latin for "coming."

WHAT IS WINTER SOLSTICE

That person who is always pointing out Christmas isn't Jesus' real birthday is also the person saying true Christmas is the pagan holiday of Winter Solstice. If you ask them what Winter Solstice is, then you might make them stumble because Winter Solstice has its own complications.

"Solstice" is made up of two Latin words: sol (sun) and sistere (to stand still). Put them together, and the word essentially means that the sun stands still. It happens around December 21 or 22, and in the ancient world, it meant that the hard winter was over and spring was on the horizon. They were basically celebrating the start of a new, better, year when everything would be warmer and more livable.

While gods were honored during the Solstice, each culture had its own interpretations. That's where all this pagan stuff came from. In Rome, for example, there was a holiday to celebrate Saturn, the god of agriculture. Germans worshiped Oden during this time. While every culture had varying celebrations, there actually is a god (Sol Invictus) that is celebrated on December 25.

So, while your Debbie-downer friend is right in that there probably was some pagan stuff at the original Winter Solstice celebrations, they are wrong in thinking that it was purely a pagan celebration. Many people probably didn't celebrate gods at all—they were just happy that hard times were over and the new harvest was coming. It was kind of like their New Year.

The Christian leaders of the time didn't stand together at a table and say, "Hey, you know how we can whip those pagans into shape and make them believers? By taking away their celebration and making them celebrate Christmas instead." If anything, they did it to be accommodating so they wouldn't have to leave their culture behind.

THREE

THE HOLY LISTICLE

We all have that uncle. The one that says crazy things. Who always seems to be getting into trouble. Who makes you cringe a little (or a lot) at their political ideology. Maybe you are that uncle!

Think about sitting with your family at a get-together. It's nice. It's intimate. People are bonding. And then that person says something that makes everyone just a little uncomfortable. That's the uncle I'm speaking of.

And chances are they're at that Christmas table because family is the one thing that follows us for life. As much as we sometimes wish we could erase them, they keep popping up in our lives, reminding us that there is blood between us.

I had more than one of those "uncles." They could be cringe-worthy. I remember sitting at the kids' table and those uncles coming over to share something that was ridiculously boring and unimportant to my young life. One uncle, in particular, would recount wildly inappropriate stories about some of his misadventures in New Orleans during Mardi Gras. They were over the top and contained situations that the 7-year-old me didn't fully understand, and the grown man me would get embarrassed by.

Black sheep also come in the form of history—the things that you don't say when the family is together. The things we want to forget. That one incident that's most definitely unhealthy to repress, and yet that's what we do.

The incidents are usually dark.

Growing up, there was a family member who was outright banned from some family gatherings because of accusations of something that happened. Half the family believed it, and half the family did not.

As a kid, I never got the full story but was always sternly warned to stay far away from him.

I thankfully was never in a room alone with the individual, but five minutes in conversation with him, and you could see through his eccentricities and vulgarities that the rumors about him were almost definitely true.

There was one time in particular when he showed up at a family gathering, and chaos ensued.

I had a pretty average family. There wasn't a lot of drama. It was the first time I saw the magnitude of how the person had affected members of the family; it was like watching people relive childhood trauma. Seeing their tears—seeing the way they shook at the sight of him—it was clear that this wasn't some fabricated story; I didn't understand how family members could just ignore things and act like nothing happened.

It's unfortunate that most families have pains like that. They put a strain on relationships, but no matter how much we want to get rid of them, we can't because we are entangled in a bloodline.

Even if we ban them from gatherings. Even if we swear not to mention their name. Even if they are physically removed from society as we know it and put in prison. They are always there. They are always that person that put a damper on our family story.

But what does all this have to do with the Christmas story?

In Jesus' day, the family wasn't just the people you saw at family get-togethers. It was how you got status. In many respects, you were who your family was. That's why when people hear about Jesus, they say, "Wait! Isn't this guy the carpenter's son?" The point being, you didn't grow up to be a philosopher. You grew up to be a carpenter.

We have two genealogies of Jesus.

As has already been mentioned, Jesus is an adult in Mark and John because they are writing to different audiences. There is a very brief reference from Paul in Romans 1:3, who says that Jesus, "was a descendant of David." But that's it.

So when it comes to where Jesus comes from, we have two stories. One in Matthew and one in Luke.[77] The purpose is intentional: to show that Jesus was more than a carpenter's son. He came from the succession of David, and therefore could rightfully claim his kingdom. It also helps cement the

[77] Matthew 1:1-16 and Luke 3:23-38

fact that Jesus Christ is not a myth or legend. He is real. He comes from a respected family line.

The list is identical from Abraham to David, but they branch off after that. There's a lot of debate in this gap. It's really best summed up by looking at the purpose of the authors. Luke is a historian. He's trying to be as accurate as possible. Matthew is writing to a predominately Jewish / Christian audience. It's also extremely likely that Matthew's draws from the line of Joseph's, and Luke's draws from the line of Mary's.

For the purpose of Christmas, however, Matthew's is more appropriate. It's appropriate because it is the black sheep genealogy.

Yes, like our family, Jesus had black sheep. And so we come to the Bible, and there's a refreshing aroma of darkness in the genealogies—refreshing in the sense that we are not alone. Even Jesus had a dark past. And the Bible's not afraid of hiding it.

That darkness is unusual. The history that Matthew gave is *not* the history that people typically gave. In fact, it's the history that people *never* gave.

If you wanted to give a family history—at least in the time of Christ—you gave an account of fathers. Women didn't define you back then. But when you look at Jesus' genealogy in Matthew, there are five women. It may not seem shocking today, but 2000 years ago, this was huge! But there's more: many of these women were gentiles! If you are trying to put together a list of family history to impress people, these are exactly the people you want to leave out.

Not to sound like an infomercial here, but that's not all! In case you need a reminder, Tamar's claim to fame was tricking her father-in-law into having sex with her! And Rahab was perhaps one of the most famous prostitutes who ever lived—and, as if you need icing on the cake, she was a Canaanite, which was not a highly regarded tribe in Jewish history.

There's one other very important distinction about these five women, however—something that was just a little off. They all had what you might call an irregular union. These are basically five women who took control of a situation and made bold moves. In that sense, we see how God controls history—how even when things don't go as expected, goodness will still come.

So to a Jew reading Matthew's genealogy, they're going to start seeing something that we frequently miss: this genealogy is messed up! These are outsiders. These are sinners. These are the very definition of black sheep.

And this obviously begs the question: what on Earth are prostitutes and adulterous women doing in this Nativity story?! This goes horribly in the church Christmas pageant. Little Timmy is not supposed to stand in front of the church in his oversized robe and voice not yet cracked to tell the audience that the Christ child has been born—and there are some prostitutes in the family. It's just not very Christmasy.

And while it is indeed best not to have little Timmy staging a reenactment of Jesus' cousin Tamar, the message of Matthew must not be lost: Jesus Christ did not come for the Jews, or the gentiles, or the kings and heads of state…he came for all of us. He came for the prostitutes, the teachers, the philosophers, the garbagemen—all race and creed. We are all equal.

The thing about this true Christmas story that we have to understand is that it's not about family and self-improvement and reflection. Yes, we come together and do family things. But that's not the true Christmas. True Christmas is about one thing and one thing only: God's love for us through gifting us with a savior born to the world.

There's one thing that's always clear in the Bible: families can be messed up. God doesn't say hug it out with the uncle who assaulted you; high-five the parent that got physical with you; bond with the people who abused substances and messed up a part of your childhood.

People confuse forgiveness with forgetfulness. Forgive, yes. Absolutely forgive! Forget? No. Forgetting forgets the healing. It tries to put a Band-Aid on a wound that needs stitches. The genealogy of Jesus shows that even the holiest of bloodlines had drama, and they were not ignored. They were remembered. There were lessons even in the darkest of times.

God uses even these dark moments in our family line for his goodness. He uses them to say bad things happen to good families (and bad), but that doesn't mean he's not there. That doesn't mean he won't heal us. Out of a line full of disgraces came a child who was God. It is the ultimate story of redemption—how God will bring us out of our family's dark moments. And how he loves each and every one of us.

FOUR

LET'S TALK ABOUT SEX...OR THE LACK THEREOF

We really can't talk about the true nature of Christmas without talking about sex. If it makes you blush a little to read a Christmas book with the naughty three-letter word, then just replace every instance of the word in the text that follows with "frickle-frackle."

Depending on your religious upbringing, the virginity of Mary is probably either not a big deal or one of the most important things to what you believe—second only to the resurrection of Christ; you walk into their house, and you'd think it was a shrine to her—candles and illustrations of her everywhere you turn.

Regardless of where you stand with regard to Mary, you probably believe that she is a virgin. But why does it matter?

And while you're thinking about her virginity, question what virgin means. That she's a pure young woman—not necessarily a virgin; that she had sex but did not have sex to have Jesus; that she was a virgin before Jesus, but not one after; or that she was always a virgin. And what about Joseph? Did he matter at all? Could Mary just as easily have married Joe the Plumper to the same effect?

So to sum up the above paragraph: the virginity of Mary isn't as simple as we are taught in Sunday school.

THE BASICS OF VIRGINITY

Taking the position that Mary was a virgin, let's consider why. Why is this important? The three common points are these:

1. **Jesus is not man-made.** If Joseph was his sperm father, then Jesus isn't exactly divine. He is 100% of man. If Mary is a virgin, then this is only 50% true. Half of him comes from man; the other half comes from God.
2. **The sin of man.** We are born with sin through the sins of our father. You basically inherit sin from good old day by this theology. Virgin birth takes away this element. Jesus does not inherit sin and is there for born sinless.
3. **Human sacrifice.** It was customary in those days to sacrifice an animal—a pure animal such as a lamb. By having no sin himself, Jesus was essentially the perfect human sacrifice. He was the only person who could offer themselves as a human sacrifice.

We'll dig more into why Mary had to marry Joseph and not Joe the Plumper in the next chapter. But looking at the above, we can start to understand why when we say "virgin," we mean virgin in the sense that we know virgin today—that she didn't do the old frickle-frackle with Joseph. If you want to make theology a little messy, you can start thinking about if that means she was a virgin for life, but this is a Christmas book, so let's keep the sex simple.

THE ELEPHANT IN THE ROOM

So let's discuss the real elephant in the room. Virgin birth seems pretty darn important. I've never meant a virgin birther, and I bet you haven't either. So why don't John, Mark, and the epistles talk about it?

Did they not know about it? Because it's hard to believe that they wouldn't—it's a pretty big deal. And if they really didn't know about it, then is it fair to assume that Matthew and Luke just made it up?

First, it's important to note one thing: they don't deny virgin birth, they just don't include it.

Not to keep reiterating this point, but the audience is really key to understanding the lack of its inclusion. Chances are the readers did, in fact, know about the virgin birth, so there just wasn't any reason to include it. Their goal of writing the book was to cover his ministry, not his birth.

While John does not specifically say it, he does very much imply that Joseph is not Jesus' father. In John 8:14, it says:

> "You are doing the works of your own father.' 'We are not illegitimate children,' they protested. 'The only Father we have is God himself.'"

What does that mean? It means the Jews knew that Jesus had the juiciest little secret:[78] Jesus was an illegitimate child.

What we do have is two very clear accounts of Mary's virginity. But what we also have is two very different accounts of that story.

In Matthew's account, adultery is on the table. He does not try to hide the fact that people will obviously be thinking this, and he wants to be one hundred percent crystal clear to the reader: that this was not the case—this is true virgin birth that we are talking about. Mary did not cheat on Joseph.

That's not the case in Luke. All eyes are on Mary in Luke. All over the Luke account, we have women—it's fair to say that Luke is far more female-centric than Matthew. Even when women aren't the main characters, they are there to complement the male counterparts. He could have easily left them out—but he didn't.

But to Joseph, in particular, there's something interesting about how Luke portrays him. Luke never tells the reader how Joseph found out about Jesus or how he feels about it; there's no angel talking to Joseph and convincing him that this is all God's will. Joseph is kind of a minor character. Luke's emphasis is on showing how women played a quite vital role in the Nativity story.

---

[78] That apparently was no secret at all.

Contrary to Luke, in Matthew's account, Joseph plays a pretty big role. Mary is there, but she almost feels lesser. Jesus is obviously the main character, but Matthew's special emphasis makes even Jesus feel like a minor character. His account is all about the genealogy—about establishing Jesus' place in history.

The theme of Matthew is simple: Jesus is the new Moses. A new covenant has rolled into town. And it all starts with this virgin birth. Without the virgin birth, the covenant would look a whole lot different.

FIVE

A LITTLE DITTY ABOUT JOSEPH AND MARY

We've spent the past three chapters thinking about theology. I hope it's been a hoot. But stories aren't driven by theology—they're driven by people. So before journeying along the sleigh ride that is Christmas, let's take a detour down the familiar street named Joseph and Mary.

I'm sure you know all about them. Maybe you even played them in the church play.

Mary's the innocent little virgin who does no wrong; and Joseph is her righteous husband who stands by her side.

But that's only a small part of the story. There are a lot of layers to these two characters.

Think about who you are. That job you have—that spouse you've chosen—even that car you drive—all of it is because your parents influenced you in some way. Some of us had fantastic relationships with our parents; others had relationships that we'd rather forget. But we can't forget them because good or bad they had a huge impact on our life—every decision we make can be linked back to a value they taught us (or in some cases, didn't teach us) in some way.

The problem with how we often think about Mary and Joseph is we see them more linear—what they did; we don't think of them in terms of what they most certainly taught Jesus.

Jesus was part human. While his God nature was unchanged, his human nature was influenced by actions in the same way as you and I. Small changes to how he was raised, and he may have ended his life not on the cross, but on the crown of Rome.

Who were Joseph and Mary in terms of the values that we can assume were passed down to Jesus?

JOSEPH: A MAN OF FEW WORDS

For years, I thought of Joseph as a widower with kids; that absolutely may have been the case, but it also absolutely may have not.

The Bible says nothing of Joseph's age, kids, or past marriages. And yet, that's what many of us think. Where does that come from?

Around 150AD, there was a book published called "Gospel of James" (also known as the "Protoevangelium of James" and sometimes the "Infancy Gospel of James").[79] A lot of

[79] Never heard of them? I recommend checking out *The New Testament Apocrypha*; there are several versions floating around. It is

early Christians had a problem with how Joseph is presented in the Bible. When early Christians had problems with something in the Bible, they turned to God, right? Some did.

Many Christians, however, were not too different from Christians today—they had a problem, so they just twisted and bent things a little to make things work in their favor. So in the case of the problem with Joseph, they just wrote a solution and passed it around as fact. The Gospel of James was one such solution.

What was the main "Joseph problem"? There were actually two. The Bible said:

1. Jesus had brothers and sisters.
2. Jesus was Joseph's son.

How exactly is that a problem? Some Christians did not want to accept that the mother of Jesus would have sex; so the James gospel fixed this by saying she didn't—Joseph just had some excess baggage from a previous marriage, and the wife had died. The other problem was many Christians didn't understand why the Bible said Jesus was the son of Joseph and the son of God. Apparently, they never heard of adoption?

Over the years, there were many legends about Joseph to accommodate these issues. At one point, good old Joseph is a 90-year-old widower who casts lots to win Mary,[80] who is 12 years old; being the respectable man that he is, he waits until

---

essentially old, non-canonical writings—mostly writings that came many years after Jesus died.

[80] Um, gross!

she is a little over 14 to marry her.[81] And he ends up dying at the ripe old age of 111.

Some also forgot about all that angel stuff and concluded that he divorced Mary, after all.

If you're grossed out by any of that, remember he was just a gentle old man caring for a 14-year-old—there was no hanky-panky going on. Nothing weird at all about a 90-year-old taking care of a 14-year-old who is carrying God's child, right?

Any dad is going to tell you, wrong! I may be stretching it here, but God's sending his one and only son into the world—I think he can find a better provider than a 90-year-old man!

But let's not debate who Joseph was (or wasn't); let's look at what the Bible says about him.

THE BIBLICAL JOSEPH

In terms of Biblical Joseph, we have two main sources: Matthew and Luke. John and Mark do reference him, but it's very short; the gospels basically say Jesus was Joseph's son, but that's it.

So what does Matthew say? In 1:18, Matthew writes:

> His mother Mary was pledged to be married to Joseph, but before they came together, she was found to be pregnant through the Holy Spirit. Because Joseph her husband was faithful to the law, and yet did

[81] Like I said, gross!

> not want to expose her to public disgrace, he had in mind to divorce her quietly. (NIV)

So from that passage, we know that Joseph was engaged to Mary, but before they had sex, Mary was conceived by the Holy Spirit; Joseph doesn't know about the Holy Spirit stuff, so he figures Mary has just been unfaithful. Being a good guy, he's decided he's just going to divorce her quietly, so her sin isn't exposed. Matthew 1:19 goes further and calls him a "righteous man" telling us that he's a good Jew who respects the Jewish law.

Before he can act on his plan, Matthew 1:20 tells us that an angel came to him in a dream and told him that Mary would give birth to God's son. So Joseph jumps on board and decides not to divorce Mary.

Both Matthew and Luke tell us that Joseph is from the line of King David.[82] That's going to be important, but let's come back to it.

Several places reference Joseph's occupation as a carpenter, but there's some debate about what this means. We (and 100s of years of art) think of carpentry as woodworking; the actual word could have just meant he was a craftsman. The point is the same in all cases, however: Joseph has an ordinary job. Their sons became carpenter's as well—not philosophers.

We can also conclude that Joseph is not a rich man. In Luke 2:24, he goes to the temple and sacrifices two pigeons. Why does that mean he's poor? Because Leviticus 12:8 tells

---

[82] Matthew 1:20; Luke 2:24

us that pigeons are the offering people should bring when they can't afford a lamb.

Luke 1:42 says, "Every year Jesus' parents went to Jerusalem for the Festival of the Passover." That seems to imply that Joseph did, in fact, stay married to Mary, and did not divorce as some later non-Biblical sources wrote; that's also the last we hear about Joseph. It is widely assumed that he died before Jesus began his ministry.

That's pretty much Joseph's biography in a nutshell. Nothing about being 90. Nothing about never having sex with Mary. Nothing about living to be 111—nothing about his death at all, actually.

THE JOSEPH THAT JESUS KNEW

So Joseph is a bit of a mystery. We know bits and pieces about him. And from those bits and pieces, we can begin to see who he was and why God picked him to raise his only son.

Try and put yourself in Joseph's sandals for a moment. You're getting married! Congratulations!

And then the woman you have pledged your life to tells you, "My aunt flow hasn't visited in a while, so I got a test—it turned triple positive, which the package says means I'm pregnant with God's child."

What do you do?

The Bible doesn't give a narrative of what Joseph did, but one can imagine he felt shocked—betrayed—hurt—angry. He probably felt all of those things at once.

Joseph had a few choices:

1. Bring Mary to the religious leaders and shame her. Joseph most likely paid a dowry to Mary's family to marry her, so in doing so, he also has money to gain. Money he can spend on another woman.
2. Marry her and divorce her quietly.
3. Stay with her and raise the child as his own.

Joseph is presented as a good Jewish boy; so when he finds out about Mary, he probably has some overly pious thoughts to teach her a lesson. Again, put yourself in Joseph's sandals here—maybe you don't want to outright shame her, but no one is going to fault you for not wanting to marry her. It's not what you bargained for, and there's an easy, respectable way to get out of it.

While the Bible doesn't tell us how he felt about the situation, it does tell us about one feeling he did have: compassion.

Divorcing Mary quietly doesn't sound too nice until we realize that in Joseph's day, the law was on his side—it was perfectly acceptable to turn the woman in. Some might have even called Joseph honorable for doing it. But Joseph ultimately decides that the first option isn't the right option; he has compassion. Before he knows anything about who the child is, he has already resolved that Mary has made a mistake, but he's not going to shame her and her family because of it.

When we think about Jesus, we often think that all these great teachings he gave were all his; Jesus was a great philosopher,[83] don't get me wrong. But Jesus was both human and God—and that means some of his teachings came from past experiences. So when we say that Jesus had compassion, we have to realize that this is partly because of where he came from—what his parents had taught him. His earthly father had compassion.

Once he concludes he'll divorce her quietly, God sends an angel down to give him the lowdown on what's going on. You have to wonder why God waited to send the angel. One can only assume it was because he was letting Joseph work through some internal struggle to make him more fit to be the father of his child. It's kind of how God works—yes, he absolutely could have sent an angel down before he wrestled with any of these thoughts. Just like God could send an angel to you and me to help us on our own journey. But our relationship with God relies on us being able to struggle through our faith—it makes us stronger and gives us the individuality that makes us unique.

So Joseph is going to divorce Mary quietly, and then he has this dream where an angel comes to him. And something interesting happens in this dream—something frequently overlooked: the angel calls Joseph "Son of David."

What's so interesting about the word choice? Pull out your New Testament and count how many other people the New Testament associates that phrase with. Need a hint? One other person: Jesus.

The angel is basically connecting Joseph and Jesus together with that phrase. And it's more important when you

[83] The greatest philosopher.

consider the lineage of the phrase. It's saying that Jesus (by the line of Joseph) is the rightful heir to the throne of David.

But the angel also tells Joseph that this is all happening to fulfill scripture. The angel has taken a two-prong approach to appeal to Joseph: he appeals to his pride (who he is through his lineage), and he appeals to his upbringing—he's an upstanding religious figure who would see the importance of Jesus through scripture.

The angel made a pretty convincing case, obviously, but you have to remember that Joseph was still human. And he still lived on Earth. He knew the consequences of marrying Mary. It didn't matter that she was literally carrying the Son of God in her womb. Society would look at this unwed couple and would cast their judgments. The Bible doesn't say this, but considering the way culture at the time was, you have to figure that for the rest of their life, the family was marked as second-class citizens.

The compassion that Jesus shows to adulterous women may very well stem from how his own mom was treated.

The Bible also tells us that Joseph made a very hard decision not long after Jesus was born: he took Mary and Jesus and went from Bethlehem to Egypt. Bethlehem to Egypt isn't exactly a walk in the park. It doesn't say what part of Egypt they went to, but let's just pretend it's the bord t's a 300+ mile journey. Walking 12 hours a day, t about 10 days…with an infant and a wife from giving birth in a manger.

Why does Joseph leave his friends and family—basically everyone he knows—to go 300 miles across the desert[84] to a land he knew nothing about? Because God told him to in a dream.

If there was one word that defined Joseph, it would be this: faithful.

It was another lesson that he passed down to his children: when God tells you to do something, you do it.

Perhaps one of the most lasting lessons, however, was the fact that Joseph was not a rich man; God provided, but that was really it. Think about Jesus' ministry if he would have been raised in a rich household. The lifestyle that Jesus preached—one without material possessions—was probably one of the easier ones for Jesus. It's how he was raised.

After Jesus visits the temple with his parents at the age of twelve, we don't see Joseph again. It's assumed that Joseph died somewhat young. While we don't know what happened, we can assume that this may well have been the first real case of suffering that Jesus experienced.

My grandpa was a man of few words. He was in World War II, but never spoke of it; he had lived through the depression, but that never came up; he had many jobs, but you never heard about them.

And yet, I learned a lot from the way he lived. From his subtle actions. He didn't tell me how to do something, he showed me.

I'd like to think that's how Joseph was. He was probably pretty average and led a simple life. But that's what Jesus

---

-h wasn't exactly a cheap trip.

needed. He was part God, so he inherently had that philosophy stuff down. What he didn't have down was the human stuff. He needed a dad who was like you and me—devotedly average.

In writing, there's an old phrase: show don't tell. When people open a work of fiction, readers don't want to read an explanation—they want to see it—they want action. That phrase—show don't tell—it applies to life as well. People thrive most when they are shown things—not told things. I think that's the life that Joseph gave Jesus; when Jesus came to him and asked a question, Joseph probably took him to his workshop and showed him in the simplest terms.

It's the same thing that Jesus applied to his own ministry. When people asked him a question, he didn't give them an answer—he gave them a parable. Where other philosophers would give a lofty narrative, Jesus gave a story—he showed them the answer.

MARY: THE MOTHER WHO KNEW BEST

Mary is almost as mysterious as Joseph, but you wouldn't know that from history. Many legends have formed around Mary as well. Some of these legends have become canonical—meaning certain churches subscribe to them as fact.

Many Catholics, for example, hold that Mary did not die. She was assumed into heaven. Some say she was a virgin for lifer. And there's even some that say that not only was Mary a virgin, but her mom was a virgin as well—because, according to people who subscribe to this theology, Mary couldn't have original sin to give birth to Jesus. In Islam, Mary is considered the greatest woman in history.

According to some apocryphal stories, Mary could walk at six months; was sent into the wilderness by the high priests, only to return unharmed. If you believe the apocryphal book *Pseudo-Matthew*, she even comes face-to-face with dragons!

Fortunately, we don't have to rely on the Apocryphal to know about Mary.

THE BIBLICAL MARY

So what does the Bible say about Mary? Like Joseph, not a whole lot. If we are to believe the customs of the time, we can assume that Mary probably was pretty young. Women in these days got married around 14 to 20.

Mary may have been attended to by angels, but we can still assume that she probably felt shaken and powerless. After the angel tells her what's going to happen, the first thing she says in Luke 1:34 is, "How can this be?"

Mary, in many ways, shows us the right way to be obedient: doubt and trust God. Just because Mary is obedient, doesn't mean she's fully on board with the decision. Faith here—and faith in our own lives—happens in stages. Mary never says, "Yes! Let's do this thing!" And she definitely doesn't say, "I get it, God! I completely understand!" To walk with God isn't to understand God; to walk with God is to trust God. The faith that comes organically happens in stages over time.

While there is a school of thought that presents Mary as sinless as well, the Bible does not seem to lean that way.

Mary, for example, refers to God as "my savior" (Luke 1:47); if you're sinless, you don't exactly need a savior to save you from your sins.

Luke shows Mary's lineage from the line of David, much like Joseph.

John 2:1-11 mentions her at the Wedding at Cana telling Jesus to do something about the wine, which has run out; John mentions her again as being present at the cross.[85] And finally, Acts mentions her as being in the upper room with the disciples after the Ascension.[86]

And that's Mary in a nutshell. We don't know when she died, although it is widely believed that John cared for her.

Her only act outside the Nativity story is telling Jesus what to do (see the box for an expanded explanation of this). The fact that she's in the upper room shows that she must have been held in high regard by the early believers. She may not be mentioned in the New Testament often, but she was obviously close to Jesus' inner circle.

THE MARRIAGE AT CANA

Like everything in the Bible, the Marriage at Cana (John 2:1-11) has a lot to be interpreted. In 2:3-5, John says:

When the wine was gone, Jesus' mother said to him, "They have no more wine."

[85] John 19: 25-27
[86] Acts 1:14

"Woman, why do you involve me?" Jesus replied. "My hour has not yet come."

His mother said to the servants, "Do whatever he tells you."

What is going on here? Mary is coming to Jesus and asking him to do something about the wine. We can assume that she knows he's capable of miracles at this point, but the miracle isn't important.

Miracles are easy. They're flashy. People read them and they think that's why Jesus is God. It's not. Lots of people did miracles. Try to get into the habit and reading beyond the miracle and looking at the meaning of it. Jesus performed lots of miracles. If John (or any gospel writer) is sharing one, then there's a reason—they haven't picked it because there's only a handful to pick from—they have picked it for a very specific reason.

So what's the reason here? Think about weddings you've gone to. If they run out of food or drinks, who do they talk to? The groom. Or the groom's father. It's their responsibility to take care of it.

When Mary comes to him and says, "They're out of wine. Do something." It's as if she is treating Jesus like the groom. Kind of weird, right? That's why it's important to look beyond the miracle. John didn't write about this miracle because it's pretty awesome—he added it because it's symbolic.

Throughout John, there's this image of Jesus as the groom. It's the idea that we can have an intimate union with God. So when Jesus says not to involve him because his "hour has not yet come," this isn't just about some flashy miracle. When he says that his hour has not yet come, it becomes clear that this isn't Mary asking him to do a miracle. This is about Jesus being called to begin his ministry by his mother.

This is likely a pretty large wedding. Lots of people. Probably prominent people. Mary knows who Jesus is. She's looking around at all these people and probably thinks, "this is the perfect time for Jesus to reveal himself."

When Jesus essentially tells Mary no, he's not saying no because he doesn't want to do the miracle—he's saying no because he doesn't want to start his public ministry.

There are lots of ways you can interpret this, given what happens next. Jesus does the miracle. Does that mean that his public ministry has begun? Maybe. But maybe not.

You could read this story and say, "God has a plan, but can alter that plan when we ask."

But you could also read it as Jesus did the miracle, but it was clear that he wasn't starting his ministry. In fact, it appears that he did the miracle largely in private. The disciples seem to have seen it, but no one else.

THE MARY JESUS KNEW

Think of yourself at 16. Maybe you weren't a rebel hanging out past 1am and doing drugs; but I can say with almost certainty that you weren't exactly ready for adulthood. You were mature. You relied on your parents more than you probably cared to admit.

Mary, at 16, seems like a senior. She's mature beyond her age. Mary didn't marry a wealthy man. Unlike what we might know today, in Jesus' day, you married who you were: rich married rich; poor married poor. So we know Mary is at the bottom of the social ladder, and now she's pregnant with someone else's baby—it really does get much lower than that. But Mary accepts it with obedience. The Mary that Jesus knew was a woman who became an adult much too quickly but had a maturity level that showed she was up for the task.

As Jesus went into the wilderness before his ministry began, he may have had a pep talk with Mary, who told him that having faith did not mean being free of doubt. Mary likely carried nine months of doubt—nine months of people asking about the baby's father; Mary was human, and the way humans rationalize what is right is with doubt. So Jesus is out in the wilderness, and perhaps one thing on his mind is Mary telling him that it's okay to question everything—to doubt everything because it's going to build him an armor that will protect him from any spiritual attack.

We don't know a lot about what Mary teaches Jesus, but one can assume she did have a "talk" with him.

Get your mind out of the gutter—not that "talk." The other "talk." The one about making hard choices—about putting God above all else. It's the choice that Mary made. She didn't rejoice at the idea of being shamed for having a baby outside of marriage; we look at Mary as a saint today, but to those who knew her, there was nothing saintly about her. She knew she made the right choice, and yet years of stares and whispers must have impacted her greatly.

And so, when Jesus comes to the garden of Gethsemane near the end of his life and throws himself on the ground in prayer, Jesus isn't rejoicing in this choice either; perhaps he's thinking of his mom—someone who knew the pains of doing God's will. But he is going to take the "cup" because it is God's will (Matthew 29:39; Mark 14:36). Jesus was a man who was raised in a home that knew more than anyone else what it meant to do God's will—that God's blessing in heaven could mean man's curse on Earth.

RAISING A CHILD OF GOD

There are children in all of our lives that we influence. The greatest responsibility obviously falls to parents. But each of us—uncles and aunts, grandparents, cousins, even neighbors—we are all shaping the children around us. We all have a responsibility to be like Mary and Joseph. To pass lessons down to the children around us.

We look at Jesus and think: of course he's like that! He's God! But that's only part of the equation.

Jesus didn't become who he was because he was God. He became who he was because he had parents who taught him the life lessons that he would go on to create a ministry around.

Christmas is the perfect time to look at all the children around us. To look at them and think about Jesus. Think about how he had people in his life that made him who he was. Think about your own actions—think about how you can show, not tell, these children lessons that they'll carry with them in life.

SIX

THE SUPPORTING CAST

Mary and Joseph are basically the starting lineup of the Nativity story. In the grand scheme of Christmas, Mary and Joseph make the all-star team, but there's still a cast of characters that help them play the game. This chapter will cover that cast of bench warmers. If you are reading the Bible, don't blink, or you'll miss them, but without them, Christmas just wouldn't be the same.

Notably absent from this chapter will be the Wise Men and Shepherds. This is an ensemble cast that deserves its own chapter.

SIMEON: THE MAN WHO LIVED LONG ENOUGH TO SEE GOD'S PROMISE

Characters aren't just put in the Bible. They are all there to teach us a lesson. So when you read Bible stories, you can read them at face value, but if you want to learn from them, you have to think about all the layers. Who are the characters and what is God trying to reveal through them—it's in people, after all, that God reveals the truth.

That brings us to Simeon. At face value, the story of Simeon and Anna is a curious one. They almost seem like filler material. But filler material doesn't exist in the Bible.

So that makes us ask: why does Simeon matter? He is being used to reveal God's promise, sure. But the fact that his name[87] is revealed is important. God wants us to know Simeon. He's showing us a life that's worth learning from.

What can we learn? Patience. Simeon lived waiting. Waiting for the Messiah. He has been told he would come by the Holy Spirit, but he's an old man, and the Messiah has not yet come. He could have questioned that it would actually happen in his lifetime—that he had spent his entire life waiting for something that would never come…and maybe he did question it every now and then. But the key here is he came. Simeon teaches us that promises come on God's time and not ours. We have to patiently await the arrival of what has been promised.

Simeon is also here for another important reason: he is being used to teach Mary her role in the world. She isn't Jesus' mom—she is the Messiah's mom.

---

[87] Simeon means "God-receiver."

ANNA: THE OLD WOMAN WITH A HEART OF GOD

In Jesus' day, you didn't have malls, snowboarding, or biking. You had Temple. Going to Temple was the big family outing.

Most people went more as a duty only during important holidays because they had other work to do throughout the rest of the year. But there were also people like Anna. Anna went to church daily. She was an elderly woman who treated the Temple how some people treat public libraries—she loved to learn, but she didn't have a wallet to buy every book on the NYT bestseller list; the Temple was basically Anna's library—she probably would have loved to own her very own copy of the scrolls, but that was not a luxury she could have, so she headed down to the Temple court and listened to the promises of the Bible being read out loud.

Because she visited so often, the priest no doubt knew who she was. So when Mary and Joseph made their way down to the Temple with their baby, Simeon probably saw her outside and knew if anyone was going to fully understand God's promise, it was going to be her.

Anna had absolutely every excuse to just stay home. She was old. She had led her life. It was time to let others care for her and to pass down her knowledge to them. But she didn't do that. She went down to that Temple every day. Her reward was to see the child that God had promised.

God rewards the devoted.

HEROD THE SOMETIMES, BUT NOT REALLY, GREAT

Every Christmas story needs a villain. Herod fits that description to a "v"—capital V, actually—because Herod wasn't just a villain, he was a super-villain. He's right up there with Hitler in terms of complete monsters with a fetish for persecution. He beat Hitler, however, in that on top of being a monster, he was actually a pretty smart guy who accomplished a lot.

Here's what we know about Herod. He came to power like most spoiled kids: his dad, Antipater. His dad had a good relationship with Julius Caesar. His dad was appointed by his good chum Julius Caesar to handle public affairs of Judea; good old pops then appointed Herod as the governor of Galilee (he later became ruler of Judea and got the moniker "King of the Jews").

He was also nicknamed, Herod the Great. You don't get a nickname like that without having some greatness behind you.

His first real political claim to fame was governing Galilee; it wasn't long before he added Syria to his list; and finally made king of Judea by the Roman Emperor, Augustus. As so often the case with rulers, Herod was paranoid—everyone and everything was out to get him, and he was not afraid to kill off people who stood in the way of his greatness—even people who were otherwise innocent.

Josephus, one of the greatest historians of this time, described him as a "great barbarity toward all men equally." So on the bright side, he wasn't a racist.

Herod was not a warm and fuzzy dude. Josephus records that he killed his wife and several of his sons; and that's just Herod's family! On his deathbed, he had a small wish: kill local leaders upon his death? Why? Because he was haunted by the thought that he would die and there would be no mourning; he wanted to make sure there was wailing on the streets when he died—never mind that they weren't wailing for him.

The thing about Herod was he achieved a lot…but he achieved it in the worst way possible. He was responsible for rebuilding the Temple in Jerusalem, and building fortresses, aqueducts, and theaters—basically returning the land to its architectural greatness. If you went up to a random person on the street and asked what they thought of him, they'd probably reply, "Oh, Herod's a great king! Terrible, terrible person, but great king!"

To Christians, Herod is, of course, most remembered for how he responded to Jesus' birth. He says he wants to go worship him, but this is just what he says to get people comfortable. His real interest in Jesus is he sees him as a possible threat to his throne, so he wants him dead (see sidebar below on the "Massacre of the Innocents").

We don't know the exact reason that Herod plays so predominantly in the Matthew account, but it's hard to overlook the fact that it is because of Herod that Jesus and his family hightailed it to Egypt.

Throughout the Christmas story, we keep seeing parallels between the Nativity story and the Moses story. I don't think it's any coincidence that to establish God's new covenant, he takes his people out of Egypt to the promised land; to establish his new covenant through Christ, he is essentially taking his promised people back to Egypt. It's as if God is cementing that this new covenant is for all people—not his promised people.

MASSACRE OF THE INNOCENTS

Matthew[88] tells us in 2:18 that Herod was pretty annoyed that he had been outwitted by the Wise Men[89] so he gave orders to kill all the boys in Bethlehem who were two years old and under.

The problem with this account? Many scholars doubt it happened. The problem is Josephus, who is sort of the go-to guy for scholars studying the history this period, doesn't mention that the so-called *Massacre of the Innocents* happened.

Josephus wasn't a member of Herod's fan club. *Antiquities of the Jews* records many of the events of early Christians and Herod's activities. It spans 20 books, thousands of pages, and hundreds of thousands of words. Three of the books were about Herod's reign. And yet it somehow overlooked this bloodbath massacre of babies? Maybe the scholars are right, right?

What you have to consider, however, is Bethlehem isn't exactly New York City. A lot of people lived there, but it was

[88] Only Matthew records this.
[89] Apparently he failed to understand the meaning of the word 'Wise Men'?

still relatively small. At the time, there probably were no more than a dozen babies that matched Herod's infant slaughter wish list. So while this was, no doubt, a disturbing and ruthless act, Josephus may have simply not included it because, in the grand scheme of Herold's reign, it simply wasn't significant enough. It's equally possible that he simply had not heard of it, because, again, Bethlehem wasn't exactly a big-time town.

While not all scholars agree that the *Massacre of the Innocents* took place, most do agree that Herod was one paranoid nut job—so it certainly fits his MO.

ZECHARIAH: THE PRIESTLY DAD

The first thing you have to realize about Zechariah, who was the father of John the Baptist, is he was married to Elizabeth.

Why is that important? It's important because she's mentioned at all. Even when women aren't predominate characters in a story, they are being mentioned. It may not seem very unusual to us today, but for the time, it was odd. Men were important to the stories—women weren't even footnotes.[90]

I believe Luke is trying to show that women had a place in the church. For thousands of years, they had been minor figures, but he's showing that they're part of this story as well. Women play an important role throughout the Book of Luke.

---

[90] Usually.

We know Zechariah was an old man when his wife conceived. Most agree they were probably in their 60s. And we know he was a priest. It gets a little sketchy after this.

Matthew 23:35 says:

And so upon you will come all the righteous blood that has been shed on earth, from the blood of righteous Abel to the blood of Zechariah son of Berekiah, whom you murdered between the Temple and the altar. (NIV)

Some have interpreted this as the same Zechariah; accordingly, many believe that he was killed when Herod gave the orders to kill kids, and he refused to give up his son's location. But we don't know this for sure.

But the bigger question is not how he died, but why Luke included him.

Luke is a historian. He wants to be sure the fullest picture of Christ is recorded. It seems that he wants to show that there is more to Jesus' ministry than just Jesus. He's showing that there was a man who paved the way for Jesus, and that man also came from miraculous origins.

But what if John had a carpenter father? He may have had that fiery spirit, but he wouldn't have had that dad who surely schooled him in Jewish law. Zechariah is a Temple priest—at the time, he was one of about 7,000, and he came from the tribe of Levi—the priestly tribe. The fact that he's not the high priest, but one of thousands of other priests, means he probably had another job. But the fact that he came from the tribe of Levi means we can be almost certain that John grew up knowing all those weird Jewish laws we find in the Old Testament.

With so many priests, duties were divided. This offering incense thing that Zechariah is doing when he meets the angel—this is kind of the once in a lifetime opportunity for a priest like him. You cast lots to do it because everyone wants to do it. And in Zechariah's big moment—this once in a lifetime opportunity—he hears about God's plan for him.

Zechariah, righteous as he is, also doubted. When the angel came to him, you'd think that this man of God would have absolutely no problem jumping on board with the idea of his elderly wife having a baby. But that's not the case; Luke 1: 18 says: "How shall I know this? For I am an old man, and my wife is well advanced in years." Zechariah, the holy man of God, doesn't quite believe God.

Who would Jesus be without John? And who would John be without Zechariah? John prepared people for a shift in Jewish teaching. In that sense, he prepared people for the message of salvation that they were about to hear. Who better to prepare for this shift then someone from the tribe of Levi—the tribe that Jews respected the most because of their priestly origin.

THE HEAVENLY MESSENGER

Angels are curious things. Statistically, it is believed that more people believe in angels than God—which doesn't really make sense. How do you believe in an angelic being from heaven without believing in someone who rules heaven? I'm sure there's something profoundly intriguing about the human mind, and it's unwillingness to believe something else is in control of our destiny, but that's not the point of this book, so I'll leave it at that.

There's nothing particularly wrong with believing in angels—heck, it's even Biblical!

The problem arises when we start believing in the Nicolas Cage kind of angels—i.e. the guardian angels. In other words, we start believing that God doesn't protect us, rather, guardian angels protect us. When we start believing we can get through anything because we have these little angels all around us, making sure no harm comes our way.

The Bible tells us that angels are a thing, but we interpret that and think they're warm and cuddling beings worthy of a Precious Moments collection. Somehow we've taken something Biblical and divine and slapped baseball uniforms on them to remind us that it's angels helping us win those championship games.

That's only loosely kind of sort of how angels work. *Very loosely*. There are two important things we should understand about angels:

1. They serve humans. Hebrews 1:14 says angels are: ministering spirits sent to serve those who will inherit salvation.
2. We should not worship them (Revelations 22:8—9).

That's how we should believe in Angels in a nutshell. Angels are not ceramic figures that we decorate our house with; or mysterious beings that show up at a car crash, save us and then disappear. They are people that help us.

They're actually less than humans in Biblical sense.

So when we think about the angel in the Nativity story, we need to do our best to remove this romanticized notion of angels and think about what the purpose of it is.

In terms of the Nativity story, in particular, the angel Gabriel is the person we should look at. In the Old Testament, and really throughout the Bible, he's seen as popping up to protect people. Because of this, he's received the title "guardian angel."

His name is not specifically called out in all the Christmas visits in the Nativity story, so it is not necessarily Gabriel in each of these instances, but the role is the same: to warn and protect. God is using them to communicate His will, and they are trusting him.

I've heard my share of angel stories from people. Most often, they come in the form of car angels for some reason—they either saved a person from an accident so it didn't happen, or they were there after. The thing about these stories is people focus more on divine intervention than God's will. They are excited to share how they saw an angel or an angel helped them but fail to look to the power that sent angels.

When we look at the Nativity story, we don't see that. We don't see people running around telling people about this magnificent angel they had just seen. The angel isn't even important to them: the message is.

God doesn't send angels so we can adore them and reflect on how miraculous they are. That's not the point of the angel in any of these stories. Writers aren't using them to show a miracle: they're using them to show a message. The only thing important about angels here is the message that is being given. Focus on that message.

SEVEN

OH, LITTLE TOWN OF BETHLEHEM?

I was born in Anaheim. My wife was born in Los Angeles. I don't recall either of us getting extra benefits for being born in these cities. It would be nice if Disneyland granted every child born in the city of its theme park a one-day pass, but alas, that does not happen. The only thing our parents got for giving birth in our cities of origin was a hospital bill.

It's the same story for all of us. Our birth city, for the most part, does not matter. But what about Jesus? He was born in Bethlehem. But does it matter?

While the city didn't gift every child born in the city a free donkey and manna for life, it does carry some significance.

HISTORICAL BETHLEHEM

Much of the significance centers around what Bethlehem was historically leading up to Jesus' birth. Bethlehem may not have been the biggest city, but its importance to Jews is significant.

Its name means "house of bread" in Hebrew, and it is mentioned nearly 30 times in the Old Testament. The name alone seems fitting for the birth of someone who would be the Bread of Life—but it's not just the name that makes this the ideal place for his birth.

Bethlehem is the place where Rachel died. It is also the setting of one of the Bible's rare love stories: that of Ruth and Boaz. More notably to the Jewish audience, however, Bethlehem is the birthplace to Judaism's great king: David.

David began the Jewish rule, which ultimately collapsed. Jesus was the rightful king to reestablish the Jewish rule—he was the one the prophets said would come—but he didn't come as a ruler who went to physical war; he came as a ruler who unleashed a spiritual war on people.

So while there were no fringe benefits to being born in the city, it's going to matter to the Jewish audience. They're looking for the fulfillment to prophesy, and Jesus being born in Bethlehem helps shape that.

BETHLEHEM, THE YEAR JESUS WAS BORN

So to a Jewish audience, Jesus being born in Bethlehem is a pretty big deal. But what was it like to actually be born in Bethlehem? Knowing what it was like doesn't change the course of history, but it will probably change your perspective on the Nativity story and how you read it.

When we think about Jesus being born in Bethlehem, we probably think about two things: no room at the inn and the manger. But how you think about these things is probably significantly different from how they actually were.

THE INN

I think most of us have the image of a hotel when we think about the inn that Mary and Joseph arrived at. We picture them pulling up to a Motel 6 with a No Vacancy sign on it.

It wasn't quite that exotic—it was, in fact, several steps down from that.

Perhaps your thinking, "What could possibly be a step down from a Motel 6?" Basically, the easiest thing to do is to forget everything you know about an "inn." In Jesus' day, the inn was more of a campground for people to roll up in their caravans. More upscale inns also had fancy two-story enclosed facilities, but even these were the type of places that made hostels look like the Ritz-Carlton.

The people who showed up at the "inns" were not the best company, and the people who took care of the inns usually had a bad reputation. As you might expect, they were not the safest places to sleep, and theft was pretty common.

What you have to wonder knowing all of this is if Mary and Joseph were really seeking to stay at an inn because the word could also be translated as "guest room." Most out-of-towners stayed with relatives in a guesthouse—not a traditional inn.

So when you read there was no room at the inn, there's a better chance that they have shown up at a relative's house only to be told there was no room for them.

When you think about it like this—when you think about that relative who rejected them—the picture becomes clearer. It *probably* wasn't a case of being no room for them at the guest house; if there really was no room, don't you think they could have made room for a pregnant woman? This was a relative, after all. I think the more realistic situation was not that there was no room at their house, rather there was no room for Mary—no room for the sinner who was carrying what the relatives considered an illegitimate child.

The thing we often miss with the Nativity story is the sheer amount of rejection Mary likely faced. Today, having a child outside of marriage isn't exactly ideal, but people don't exactly slam doors in your face—in fact, most people are compassionate to the situation. This wasn't the case then; people shunned these type of people, and the person reading the gospels hundreds of years ago probably understood this message much more clearly than we do today.

THE MANGER

So there's no room at the inn—no spare bedroom at the guest house. And they end up at the manger. What isn't in the Christmas pageants, however, was the manger might have, in fact, been the relative's home.

Perhaps, the relative rejected Mary for her unfaithfulness but wasn't so cold as to send her away entirely. So to be a kind relative, they just sent her to give birth with the animals.[91]

Most homes then had an upper and lower level. The upper level was where the family stayed—the living quarters. The lower level was where the animals were kept. If the house was extra nice, then the animals' quarters would be divided—one side for the animals and a second side where the people who cared for the animals could sleep.

If this was the arrangement, then Mary could have been in the sleeping area of the manger when she gave birth, and Joseph, who was obviously good with wood being a carpenter, would have been able to go next door to make a cradle out of the materials he found there.

The fact that they are in a manger probably also benefited the shepherds. It narrowed their search for Jesus from several homes to just the ones with mangers—which was far fewer.

It's easy to see the manger story as an "awe, poor baby Jesus" type story; I don't think that's the intention of the author. I don't think he's trying to get you to pity Jesus; it is true that nobody should have to be born in these conditions. But the bigger truth being revealed here by the author is something about his parents. It reveals that they are poor and need to rely on the kindness of others to survive. That's a lesson that Jesus no doubt will carry with him for life.

What would Jesus' message to believers be had his parents been a little wealthier? If they didn't have to rely on family? Jesus' story from his very birth is one where you need others for your survival.

---

[91] If you thought your relatives were bad, then you may relate.

His birth taught Jesus, and it teaches us, that we aren't in this life alone. It's a lot better when we have a circle of family—not family in the literal sense, but a family of believers—who we rely on for support.

Perhaps when Jesus got older, he asked about his birth story and learned what happened. But I don't picture Mary and Joseph telling him how unhappy they were with the situation; I imagine them telling him that we should always be thankful for the support that we get. I don't think they were bitter towards the relatives who couldn't make room for them—I think they loved them all the same. And these were the parents that raised Jesus—that taught him right from wrong.

A DELIVERY ROOM MEANT FOR A KING

You wouldn't be wrong for thinking that Bethlehem was chosen as the birthplace for a savior because of its historical significance, but you wouldn't be completely right either.

If it had been God's will all along to show this is the right place for a king to be born, then wouldn't you think the whole story would have been a little more…kingly? He could have given Mary a bed. He could have given them a house. He could have treated the birth as something quite royal.

He doesn't.

The birth is in a significant place with humble origins. God took a historic place, but he stripped away any possible thing that could have been interpreted as wealthy. He made Jesus the least of us, so people would never be able to say he is the

God to the well-off—he is the God to all people. We are all equal in God's eyes.

He was born in a manger to show that salvation is not something you can inherit or buy or earn. Salvation is a gift given freely, and we only need to accept it.

There is one final thing that should be considered about Bethlehem, and that is what happened after Bethlehem: Egypt.

Ultimately, Joseph takes his family to Egypt, and we should be careful to observe here the obvious parallelisms between the Nativity story and that of Moses. This is, in many ways, the reverse story of Moses. Throughout the gospels, there will continue to be obvious parallels between the Moses story and Jesus' ministry. But they start here with his birth story.

Moses is born in Egypt. Out of danger, God brings his people out of Egypt to Israel and forms a covenant with them in Israel.

Jesus is born in Israel. Out of danger, God brings his people out of Israel to Egypt and forms a covenant with them in Egypt.

Symbolically, it's like God has said I'm bringing you home.

God could have put a stop to Herod—he could have hardened his heart. But he needs Jesus' family to leave. He needs them to show that this king that has been brought into the world in the most holy of Jewish cities—he's not only for the Jews.

God sets the stage in the most symbolic city of them all—but then they flee this symbolic city, and the message should not be lost: Jesus is not going to be the king of Israel. He is going to be the king of the gentiles—of all people.

EIGHT

OH, LITTLE STAR OF BETHLEHEM?

In California, stars are something of a rarity. I suppose if I saw a star in the sky, it would be a pretty big deal because all the lights sort of dim them out and you have to go miles outside of the big cities to see them.

But once you are out in the desert, stars fill the sky. Looking at those millions of stars in the sky, it's hard not to wonder about this Nativity Star. What was so special about it?

Was God sitting on top of it with a cowboy hat riding it up and down like a wild bull ride? Because the way people have made it sound over the years makes something about it seems a little…over the top. Like no ordinary star.

It's a touching anecdote, for sure. My daughter tells me the movie that bares its name is pretty good as well.[92]

But is there more to this Star than a cozy picture book that you read to your kid each Christmas?

THE BIBLICAL STAR

What does the Bible actually say about the Star? It may surprise you. The Star usually is shown as quite—grandiose. But the Bible doesn't tell us that. Matthew 2:2 says this:

> Where is the one who has been born king of the Jews? We saw his star when it rose and have come to worship him. (NIV)

That's not exactly the fairytale most of us would expect. In verse 9, the mysterious star pops up again when Matthew records:

> After they had heard the king, they went on their way, and the star they had seen when it rose went ahead of them until it stopped over the place where the child was. (NIV)

Traditionally, the Star is seen as a guiding light—something they saw that led them to Jesus. But the idea that the star

---

[92] With Oprah Winfrey voicing a character, how could it possibly be anything but excellent? If you agree, please do not go to Rotten Tomatoes.

basically hovered brightly over the manger is probably a bit of a stretch.

THE SCIENTIFIC STAR

That wicked thing some Christians call science has also done much to prove the Star existed.[93] There are several theories about this Star being everything from a meteor to a supernova; many have said it was Halley's Comet.

The problem with any scientific theory is only some astrologers of the time documented anything. Normally, a star this bright could be seen across the world, so you have astrologists in other countries talking about it. So whatever the Star was, it was something that wasn't seen around the world. It was unique to a specific region.

Why would God go through the hassle of having a Christmas Star that couldn't be seen by the entire world? Why didn't he grab hold of a star and bring it inches from Earth's atmosphere? That certainly would have gotten our attention!

Before you answer that, you have to realize that God is not one to get our attention through force. He wants us to come to him naturally and organically.

The Star is a subtle—but powerful—message from God; he gives us what we need to see it, but it's still up to us to actually see it.

---

93 Who knew science could work with and not against Christianity?

CHRISTMAS LIGHTS

When I was a kid, we had Candy Cane Lane. We'd visit each Christmas Eve with hundreds of other cars. Slowly, we'd make our way through a neighborhood where every house was immaculately decorated.

This was the 80s—long before there were apps to put lights in sync or inflatable mascots could be easily bought at Home Depot. These people put effort into their lights—real craftsmanship. It was easy to imagine hundreds of hours of work going into the neighborhood.

Neighbors came together to make sure even the scrooge neighbor who didn't want to put up lights got involved. If someone didn't want to participate, the neighbors would do the work for them and even supply the lights.

It was the kind of neighborhood community effort not often seen today.

As a kid, I saw those lights like probably most other people: beautiful arrays of Christmas spirit. But the lights have more to them than that—probably more than most people who put them up know.

In those Christmas lights, we can symbolically see the Nativity Star. It was the light that guided the Wise Men, but it's also easy to imagine that it was the light coming into the world through Jesus.

In Genesis, God brought light into the world. Flash forward to the Gospel of John, and what do we see? John 1:1-5 says:

> In the beginning was the Word, and the Word was with God, and the Word was God. He was with God in the beginning. Through him all things were made; without him nothing was made that has been made. In him was life, and that life was the light of all mankind. The light shines in the darkness, and the darkness has not overcome a it. (NIV)

While John doesn't talk about the Nativity Star, he does talk about Jesus being the Word becoming flesh—he's basically recording the New Covenant version of the creation story. Symbolically, it's difficult not to see that Star as representing Christ bringing light into the world.

I don't think it's any coincidence at all that there was a bright star when Christ was born and darkness when he left.

As Jesus is up on the cross, Matthew records in 27:45:

> From noon until three in the afternoon darkness came over all the land. (NIV)

Light came into the world with Christ, and darkness came over the world when his spirit left him.

God isn't known for being flashy—for popping up in the sky and saying, "what's up" to everyone. He certainly could be. But it's not in God's nature to do that. He teaches us through symbolic acts and through the actions of others.

Light didn't need to come into this world. Darkness didn't need to fall upon the world. If none of that would have happened, then Jesus would still be God.

He did it, however, because He was painting us a picture of what Christ meant. He did it to visually show how He came into the world and how He left the world.

The Star was perhaps a guiding light to the Wise Men, but it was much more than the Christmas plays let on. The Wise Men, as we'll learn in forthcoming chapters, were no strangers to traveling—they didn't need a star to guide them. They knew how to get places.

So next time you are out on your Christmas light drive, enjoy them. Make it part of your annual tradition and share them with your children and grandchildren. But at some point pause as you stare at them and remember that the light of Christmas means something.

Remember that those lights aren't just pretty. Remember that they mean something. However secular that home is, the underlying message is there: God came into the world. The word became flesh.

NINE

SHEPHERD'S WATCH

How many good sermons have you heard about the shepherds? Have you heard any at all? In the grand scheme of things, the shepherds kind of seem to take a back seat to the Wise Men—you might even be sitting there right now thinking: "wait, weren't the Wise Men the Shepherds?" Heck, I wouldn't blame you because I've thought that myself.

Yes, they're romanticized in those nativity stories, but they're kind of mysterious—you finish the account, and you might think, "well, that was nice," but you aren't quite sure what to make of it.

The fact is, there was nothing very grand about the shepherds—they didn't travel from a great distance and bring lavish gifts. Their gift was their presence in some regards. But as we keep seeing, things don't happen in the Bible just because they're nice—they happen because there's something deeper than what's on the surface.

THE BIBLICAL SHEPHERDS

So what's going on with the shepherds? Why are they even here? Let's look at the Biblical account first. The Shepherds account is found in Luke 2:8-20:

> And there were shepherds living out in the fields nearby, keeping watch over their flocks at night. An angel of the Lord appeared to them, and the glory of the Lord shone around them, and they were terrified. But the angel said to them, "Do not be afraid. I bring you good news that will cause great joy for all the people. Today in the town of David a Savior has been born to you; he is the Messiah, the Lord. This will be a sign to you: You will find a baby wrapped in cloths and lying in a manger." (NIV)
>
> Suddenly a great company of the heavenly host appeared with the angel, praising God and saying,
>
> "Glory to God in the highest heaven, and on earth peace to those on whom his favor rests."
>
> When the angels had left them and gone into heaven, the shepherds said to one another, "Let's go to Bethlehem and see this thing that has happened, which the Lord has told us about."
>
> So they hurried off and found Mary and Joseph, and the baby, who was lying in the manger. When they

> had seen him, they spread the word concerning what had been told them about this child, and all who heard it were amazed at what the shepherds said to them. But Mary treasured up all these things and pondered them in her heart. The shepherds returned, glorifying and praising God for all the things they had heard and seen, which were just as they had been told. (NIV)

The shepherds at the start of this story are terrified. If you've read the Bible, then that shouldn't surprise you. Terror is a normal emotion when people are in the presence of God or something quite holy.

It's quite curious. You'd think that people seeing God would experience the opposite—a feeling of overwhelming awe and joy. But the Old Covenant created a separation between man and God, which came because of Adam and Eve's sin.

I'm sure you know all about that expression "personal Jesus" and if you are a Christian, you probably even know what it means. But this concept was completely foreign to Jews. The shepherds—or really anyone for that matter—didn't have that connection because that wasn't the God of the Old Testament.

But there's a shift here. The angel tells them to fear not! The angel is telling them that he's about to show something that's going to take away that fear. He's telling them to go look because they are about to be the eyewitnesses to the New Covenant that God has brought.

The New Covenant isn't about separation, rather closeness. When you hear people say they have a personal relationship with Christ, that's what they mean. God came to the world so we can experience that closeness that we couldn't have before.

So when the shepherds return to the fields after seeing Jesus, and they're praising God, it's not just because they have seen something miraculous—it's because they understand what he represents. It's because they are no longer afraid of God.

WHAT EXACTLY IS A SHEPHERD?

I don't think it would surprise you if I said that God picked the shepherds because this was the occupation that Jesus filled as the "Good Shepherd." The metaphor of Christ being the shepherd is one that comes up a lot. But what does that mean?

To understand the significances of the shepherds, it helps to ask: what exactly is a shepherd? If you are thinking, "someone who watches sheep," you aren't exactly wrong. But it's not the full story.

Who was the shepherd that the early readers of the Bible knew?

Shepherds were not city folk. They hung around the outside of the city. In that respect, they weren't the civilized well-to-do people that you might expect to come and worship this young child of God.

Their job was not an easy one. They had to keep sheep together, make sure there were no predators that would eat them, and keep them fed. They also had to make sure people didn't steal them—which means they were always sleeping in shifts making sure someone was always awake watching them at night.

It was not a desirable job, but it was respected for one reason: the Passover. Each year, if you wanted a lamb to sacrifice, then the shepherds were absolutely needed. Curiously, the shepherds did not go to the temple themselves because they were considered unclean.

People basically said, "Hey, we need you because we can't have salvation without you, but we don't want you in our church because you are dirty." How true is that for many Christians? Who looks at their neighbors and says, "Hey, we sure do love you—but we don't want you in our church because…well…you're sort of unclean." If only they'd stop being gay, then they'd, of course, welcome them in their church. It's the whole idea of love the sinner but not the sin.

So when a reader sees this story, what they're seeing is a savior that isn't only for the upper class. The shepherds gave an eyewitness account of the Nativity story that commoners could believe in.

Christ comes for all of us, including the lower class—the shepherd who were quite literally outsiders are the people that Christ is going to represent.

What may be overlooked by readers, however, is that was the night the shepherds found out they were about to lose their jobs. Those sheep they watch day in and day out saw the promised savior—people would no longer have to sacrifice the sheep that they protected. And they rejoiced.

The shepherds saw something in that baby that many of us never see: it's not about them—there's something greater than ourselves in Christ. They were willing to humble themselves and accept that even at the sake of losing their very profession, they were willing because the reward was worth it. They were dying to their old selves and renewed with something greater.

The Christmas message is about seeing that reward—it's about realizing that there is something greater than ourselves in that infant in the Nativity story; sometimes we get caught up in the family and gift-giving and forget the real Christmas story is about humbling ourselves and realizing we are dead to self—our old self doesn't matter: Christ matters.

TEN

WISE MEN OR JUST MEN?

When a baby is born, there are pretty much two guarantees: 1) you'll get no sleep, 2) you'll get lots of visitors.

People love babies—most people anyway. So my money is on little baby Jesus getting lots of attention. Lots of people surely came to see him.

But that's not what the Bible tells us. The Bible tells us about three:[94] the Wise Men (AKA, the Magi).

Why?

These are just three guys, right? They're wise according to their namesake. But really, what gives? Were they some kind of royalties? Just run-of-the-mill shepherds? Or were they just pretty wise guys?

Curiously, the Wise Men play a somewhat mysterious and even minor role in the gospel, but when we start to really break them down, we start to see just how pivotal they actually were. They may, in fact, be some of the most important characters in the Nativity story.

---

[94] Well, probably not three, but we'll get to this blasphemy momentarily, so bear with me.

The Matthew account of the Wise Men is probably like no pageant you have ever seen—no camels—no following a star—not even a manger! In all likelihood, there were several Magi (not three), who rode on horses (not camels) to a home (not a manger).

I'm sorry to disappoint you here, but, brace yourself, the Wise Men probably were not at the Nativity! Before you lash out at me and say, "How dare you! Hobby Lobby's ceramic nativity does not show that!" open up your Bible and tell me where it says it. In fact, the Wise Men probably came to Jesus when he was a young boy.

THE BIBLICAL WISEMEN

Who were these wise old men? The Bible doesn't exactly say.

Magi have played an important role throughout history. They appear in several different kingdoms in lots of different forms. In most places, kings and rulers retain their kingdom only with the approval of the magi. They're kind of like board members at a large corporation. There's a chairman of the board running things, but there are board members making sure that person makes the right decisions.

The story of the Wise Men is found only in the Gospel of Matthew. Matthew 2:1-12 records:

> After Jesus was born in Bethlehem in Judea, during the time of King Herod, Magi[a] from the east came to Jerusalem and asked, "Where is the one who has

been born king of the Jews? We saw his star when it rose and have come to worship him."

When King Herod heard this he was disturbed, and all Jerusalem with him. When he had called together all the people's chief priests and teachers of the law, he asked them where the Messiah was to be born. "In Bethlehem in Judea," they replied, "for this is what the prophet has written:

"'But you, Bethlehem, in the land of Judah,
are by no means least among the rulers of Judah;
for out of you will come a ruler
who will shepherd my people Israel.'"

Then Herod called the Magi secretly and found out from them the exact time the star had appeared. He sent them to Bethlehem and said, "Go and search carefully for the child. As soon as you find him, report to me, so that I too may go and worship him."

After they had heard the king, they went on their way, and the star they had seen when it rose went ahead of them until it stopped over the place where the child was. When they saw the star, they were overjoyed. On coming to the house, they saw the child with his mother Mary, and they bowed down and worshiped him. Then they opened their treasures and presented him with gifts of gold, frankincense and

> myrrh. And having been warned in a dream not to go back to Herod, they returned to their country by another route. (NIV)

People have debated for hundreds of years whether or not Herod really killed babies; one argument says that the writer added it because they wanted to make Herod look bad.

What we can know for sure is this: Herod was a crazy SOB—some say literally crazy. He was paranoid about losing power. So when he hears there's a kid born who is the rightful heir to the Jewish people—the people who make up a good chunk of his kingdom—it makes sense that he is going to get paranoid. It makes sense that he would kill a bunch of kids to protect himself from losing his throne—he was just that crazy.

WILL THE REAL WISE MEN PLEASE STAND UP?

How many Wise Men were there? I'm sure some people will say three—a lot of people will say that. But three is a made-up number. Before you wag your finger at me and scream, "heresy!" go get Biblical. Go ahead, look it up. I'll wait.

What did I tell you—never says three. It just says they were men. Could have been three. Could have been several. The reason so many people think it's three—why this is in the Nativity stories—is because they gave three gifts. So by that logic: three gifts equal three Wise Men…which just isn't true, of course.

The number three stayed relevant over the years more for logistics. It is far cheaper to make a nativity with three Wise Men than several, and it's quicker to paint a painting with three than several.

We also don't know where they came from or even who they were. Magi came from several regions, and it really can mean several things. People have said they were magicians. People have said they were kings or royalty. People have said they were priests. People have said they were lots of things.

"Wise Men" is used previously in the Bible in Daniel 2:2-10 to describe the men who helped kings understand their dreams. People were really into dreams back then.

They also most likely didn't see the infant Jesus. They probably didn't get to the manger when he was born. They most likely saw him in a house, and he was probably a toddler at this point. You have to wonder what he was doing to make them fall down and worship him. It doesn't go into detail. These weren't Jews; if someone passes them a note in gym class that outlines how this little Jesus kid is the Messiah, they'll have no idea what that means. So they probably witnessed something when they got there that made them understand that Jesus was no normal baby.

We also know that the Magi were probably in a pretty large group. That's how people like them traveled back then. They were in a caravan of people—probably full of servants and even soldiers. How large? It doesn't say. But most likely several dozen.

Because of their size, we also know they were most likely very well-traveled. They didn't need a star to guide them.

WHY THE WISE MEN

Why was it so important for the Wise Men to see Jesus? It sets the stage for his ministry. These are not Jews. These are cultured men from far away—people who perhaps don't even know what Judaism is. God is using them to say, "Guess what everybody! Anyone can have me now—I'm not the God of the Jews—I'm the God of all people."

He's also using it to show how people can believe and not have salvation. Herod believed. He believed that there was a special baby—a boy who was the rightful ruler to the Jews. And he wanted him dead. Anyone can say they believe in Christ. But that doesn't get you into heaven. Knowing him personally is what gets you into heaven.

It's important to think not just "why" when you think about the Magi, but what they actually did. They gave a model for gentiles who came after to follow:

- **They wanted to know**. They were spiritually hungry. It's the behavior of everyone out there. Even atheists wonder if there is something. We all do. There's a spiritual void in us that we seek to fill. These Magi were probably scholars, but that didn't make them stop searching to know more.
- **They obeyed**. They wanted to know and when God came to them they didn't turn away or say, "This is amazing! But we will come back when we are a little older—perhaps after we've lived awhile." They knew they were in hot water with

Herod—they knew who he was and what he did to people who weren't in his favor. But they went. They trusted a higher power, you could say.

- **They worshiped**. We'll go into this more later—what it means that they worshiped. But for now we can just accept that they saw Jesus and they knew they were in the presence of something that was beyond them.
- **They gave thanks**.

WHAT'S IN A WORSHIP?

The Magi worshiped Jesus.

Most of us read that at face value. They are basically acknowledging that this kid is divine. But that may not be the case.

What they were actually doing, really depends on what you think happened next. Worship here could have been interpreted as paying respect. It was the same thing you would do to royalty or anyone of greatness back then.

So they very well could have just been giving respect to something special they saw with the baby.

Or they could have been worshiping as we know the word today. If that was the case, then their lives would have been changed, and what they did next is more obvious.

WHAT HAPPENED TO THE WISE MEN?

The Wise Men kind of leave as mysteriously as they come. What happened to them? Did Herod find them and put them in prison? Did they just wander off into the sunset never to be seen again? Or something else.

It seems clear that the Magi didn't get what they were coming for, but they left with something they didn't expect. They were wise men indeed, but they left with the belief that wisdom wasn't exactly what they previously thought: wisdom was found in this small child.

I'm sure they came to Bethlehem expecting a palace: expecting to find this child on a throne being cared for by servants. They expected to be in the presence of traditional royalty. They didn't find that. And yet they weren't disappointed.

What they found was a child in a neighborhood that was all but royal—a child that was surrounded by what most would consider average—or more likely poor.

Jesus would later say in Matthew 19:24: "it is easier for a camel to go through the eye of a needle than for someone who is rich to enter the kingdom of God." (NIV) This is the wisdom that the Wise Men received. They were almost certainly rich men—or at the very least, used to being in the presence of rich men, who passed their lavishes onto them.

I'd like to believe that if they truly thought that Jesus was divine, then it had a lasting impact on their lives. They didn't just leave and go about their lives. They left and were changed. They put aside the lives they had lived—those of lavish riches.

Dwight Longenecker makes an interesting claim about what happened to them in his book *Mystery of the Magi*. He believes the Wise Men ended up in Damascus with the Essence and opened a school of wisdom.

That in itself isn't that impressive. It's the person who comes to study at their school that brings a great twist. Longenecker proposes that Paul, who is very much familiar with Damascus, settles there for a short time after his conversion. It is here that he is taught by the Magi about what it means to be a Christian.

Why is that interesting? Consider for a second what Paul did really well: he spoke to the gentiles. Paul had a way of taking the culture that they knew and making it relatable. He was that hip pastor who could take any movie and somehow make it a sermon.

Paul is deeply rooted in Jewish beliefs. You would think that even a converted Paul would have been very…Hebrew in his teaching. But he's not. It can very easily be argued that Paul did more for the gentiles than any other teacher of his day. He was able to do this because his teaching included a lot more than the typical Jewish teacher. He's able to see God's beauty in all things—to look at the Greek gods even and say, "God is there!"

Paul could have obviously learned these teaching from anyone, but anyone wasn't exactly teaching them. To learn these kinds of teachings, Paul really had to look for someone outside of the typical Jewish-Christian circle. He had to find a teacher who knew what these gentile people really believed. Who better than these Magi from the East?

If any of this is true, however, you do have to wonder why Matthew or Luke didn't write more about the Magi—where they went, that is. It seems like that would make a good story—especially to Luke, who introduces Paul to Christianity with the Book of Acts. This makes sense as well, however. The Wise Men, at this point, would have still been fugitives.

Even Matthew wrote about the Magi in somewhat obscure terms. A Jewish audience probably would have wanted to know what country they were from and what king sent them. That almost seems like part of the story. But you start to get the feeling that the writers are protecting the Magi by hiding truths about them.

There was also a very big trend in the early church: Gnosticism—basically the idea that some Christians could have "secret knowledge." So it probably wouldn't have exactly helped Matthew or Luke to write about the Magi—these men of the East who aren't from Jewish tradition—opening up their own school of thought. They would have sounded like Gnostics to some people. Added to this, Luke already knows that Paul is an outsider—that he faces opposition often from his Christian brothers and sisters who aren't crazy about some of his teachings. Many early Christians wanted to be Jewish but believe in Jesus—keep the good old ways if you will. That meant being a little more inclusive, and not welcoming to sinners. Paul was very much opposed to this. Luke didn't want to say, "he's opposed to it, and he was taught by these guys who were borderline Gnostics."

MORE THAN MEETS THE EYE?

So there's a strong chance that after his conversion, Paul went and studied under the Magi. But what about Jesus?

It's a little more of a stretch. But Damascus is certainly not far from where Jesus grew up. And there is a very sizable gap between when the Wise Men left and when Jesus' public ministry begins. So it's possible.

Maybe Joseph died, and Mary moved to Damascus, and the Wise Men taught Jesus about the people he would one day minister to.

There are a lot of hypotheticals here, and I'm not going to suggest more. What we know is that Jesus probably learned about the gentiles from someone. How amazing would it be if Jesus went to them for teachings, and then Paul would later do the same?

ELEVEN

THE GIFTS OF THE MAGI

So now we have a decent idea of who these three wise guys were, but I have left out what they are perhaps most famous for: the gifts. I purposefully left them out because the gifts are kind of a character in themselves—so let's dig in and unwrap them.

Perhaps you don't know what the gifts were by memory, but you surely aren't surprised when you hear their names: gold, frankincense, and myrrh.

Today we are so accustomed to those gifts that we don't really think about them. But when we stop and consider them, one thing will probably come into your head: they're weird.

When my wife and I had our daughter, we got clothes, gift cards, baby furniture. Do you know what we didn't get? Frankincense, myrrh, and gold. And if we had? We probably would have said, "Gee, thanks. This will come in handy when…well, actually, never—just set it in that pile marked 'useless.'"

Were the Wise Men the worst givers of all? The kind of men who bought their wives bowling balls for their anniversary? Or are we missing something here?

THE GIFTS AT FACE VALUE

The Bible is an epic book. It's hard not to resist making it something greater than it is—it often is greater! The problem is people sometimes take things that aren't stories, and they make them stories. This is especially true with the gifts of the Magi. We create an almost fairytale allure to them—we make them symbolic and even divine and try to say there's more to it than meets the eyes.

That's fair. A lot of things in the Bible are symbolic. But are the gifts of the Wise Men one of them? Are the gifts these grand representations—some luxurious mythological symbol of who Christ is?

You could look into the double meaning of the gifts. But first, it's important to look at the culture of the time. How would Matthew's readers interpret the gifts?

Gold, frankincense, and myrrh have a certain mystique to their name today; hundreds of years ago, however, they were essentially Middle Eastern commodities.

Today, as it was then, gold was basically an international currency. So it's easy to see how they were bringing wealth with this gift.

Myrrh was a sort of ancient pain killer; it was commonly used in battle to treat wounds—it was actually used as a pain killer during the crucifixion, but Jesus refused it (Mark 15:23).

Frankincense was also used in medicine to help with inflammation.

So before we start breaking down the gifts and say they were these grand symbolic gestures, we need to understand this: these three gifts probably represented the richest gifts the Wise Men could think to give. If they saw Jesus as royalty, then they would want to bring their best. This was their best.

These gifts probably carried some other purpose, however. Joseph wasn't exactly rolling in cash. Every dad shares a similar concern: how they are going to be able to provide. I know I had that worry. But I also had a few more luxuries that Joseph didn't have.

But there's more. A short time later, Joseph is told he has to take his family and make a run for it because they're in danger. To us, it doesn't sound so bad. If God told me I needed to drop everything and take my family from California to New York, it would no doubt be a major thing, but the journey itself wouldn't be that expensive.

That's not the case for Joseph. The journey was several days on a dangerous road. These gifts would provide him the finances needed to make such a journey.

GIFTS AS SYMBOLS

So we know the gifts were fit for royalty. Were they more than that?

Gold is a no-brainer. They gave gold as a way of saying they believed in his rule. They were honoring him with Earthly riches.

Frankincense or incense was commonly used in temple worship. It was also used to anoint priests. So symbolically, this could be the Wise Men's way of saying that they were anointing Jesus. It's problematic when you consider that the Wise Men were most likely not Jews. So it's not like they were anointing Jesus in a way a Jewish priest was anointed.

Myrrh, in addition to being used to treat wounds, was used in embalming. So in that respect, it could have been foreshadowing death or pain. Some people like to go as far as saying it symbolizes being dead to self so we can live in Christ.

Any of those symbolic gestures could indeed be true. They certainly make for nice stories and good anecdotes in sermons. Because we don't know, however, it's important to stick with the truth: the Wise Men were giving gifts fit for royalty.

The gifts, symbolic or not, were the Wise Men's way of saying this child is not just a child: this child is a king. You didn't give these kinds of gifts to someone ordinary; you didn't even give these gifts to close relatives. You gave them to kings. You gave them to honor and strike up alliances. You gave them so this king knew that you wanted a friend and not an enemy.

CHRISTMAS' TRUE GIFT

Later in this book, we'll look briefly at some of the many reasons we give gifts at Christmas. Some of it is rooted here in the gifts the Magi brought. Before we get back to our regularly scheduled gift-giving, however, let's pause and think about the true gift of Christmas.

When we read about what the Magi gave to celebrate Jesus' birth, we tend to look for the symbolism. If we look hard enough, we can find some of that—but that's not the point. What the Magi gave perhaps adds something to the story, but we can't forget the true gift of Christmas.

The true gift of Christmas isn't what they gave, but what God gave us. Isaiah 9:6 says: "For to us a child is born, to us a son is given" (NIV); Jesus is more than a savior—he is a gift we are given.

So as we pass around gifts to each other and as we think about these gifts that the Magi gave, let's remember that God is also passing a gift to us: salvation.

EPILOGUE

Christmas is a time for celebration. We all have our traditions. Some of us more lavish than others.

My parents used to give us a banana every year in our stocking; it started because they wanted to make sure our stockings looked full but continued because that's the memory we had. Even as adults, my brother and I would go to the house for Christmas dinner and seek out the banana in the stocking. I remember one year it wasn't there and my brother was devastated. He didn't need a fancy gift—he just needed a $0.29 banana. I'm pretty sure they weren't even organic.

My mom used to tell me stories about her parents wrapping silverware; they didn't have a lot of money, but they wanted their kids to have something to unwrap. They wanted them to see the gifts under the tree and know there was something to look forward to.

Christmas isn't about the gifts as much as having something to look forward to.

To a child, there's an element of wonder and surprise. Yes, it may be around a magical figure named Santa, but it's also a reminder to adults that Santa is, in many ways, symbolic of Christ. We are helping children see the wonder and surprise of Christ. How great would it be if adults could capture the same allure for Christmas as children? That would be a Christmas miracle, indeed.

Jesus' entire message was about getting people to the state of being children. Blessed are the children.

He didn't want to return us to a child state so we could get on the floor and play Hot Wheels. He wanted to get us there because it's only as children that we can abandon our fears and return to an innocent state. Kids don't worry about death. About sin. About who is saying what about them. They don't worry about tomorrow or yesterday. Kids live in the moment. They live knowing that their parents are watching over them, and nothing bad can happen.

Understanding the real Nativity story isn't about debunking all you knew growing up. It's about appreciating it even more. Knowing that there is something more that God wants to tell you. There is a child that is a reminder of Christ. That God came to us in human form. But it's important to remember that he is a child. God could have come to us as a man. He could have appeared spontaneously from the sky, and we would have been none the wiser.

You could argue that coming as a man and not a child would have made him less human—that he wouldn't have experienced the pains and understood truly what it was like to be human. That's fair. But I think there's more to it than that. He came as a child to remind us of the state we are to return to. To remind us that the goal of Christianity is salvation—but salvation is returning to that child form.

It's easy to get caught up in the overt cheesiness of the season. To say things like, "You can't have Christmas without the Christ." It's cute. But that's not Christmas. That's part of Christmas, but it's Christmas from a very one-dimensional angle.

The Christmas that the Bible teaches us is more spiritual than sensational. When you unravel the stories, you begin to see the innocence in them. How Christmas is about finding joy and worship in places where you wouldn't expect to see them. You begin to see God's gift to us and how he wants us to share that gift with the world. You can't wrap that kind of Christmas with paper—you can only wrap it with actions.

Paul, who perhaps was a student of those Wise Men, was the master of living in the world—but using it to show others the love of Christ. There is nothing in this world that cannot be used for God's glory, and that includes our Christmas traditions.

Keep your traditions. Keep your gifts.

When Winter Solstice was replaced with Christmas, it's the same approach the church took. They encouraged people to keep on keeping on. But as you keep those things, take time to dwell on the real Nativity story. And take time to act on those feelings. You don't always worship God with a prayer and a bow of thanks—you worship him by sharing his love with the world.

Think about how you can make a tradition for your family that does this—that lets you worship God together and celebrate what really happened that night in Bethlehem when Jesus was born.

APPENDIX A: MATTHEW AND LUKE COMPARISON

We've established that Matthew and Luke had very different Nativity narratives because they were writing to two different audiences for two different purposes. But that's not to say they were entirely different. Both share similarities. The below table outlines the most distinctive ones.

	Matthew	Luke
Mary and Joseph are engaged	1:18	1:27; 2:5
Mary is a virgin when she conceives	1:18, 25	1:27, 34

Mary conceives by the Holy Spirit	1:18, 20	1:35
God says his name shall be Jesus	1:21	1:31
Jesus will be a savior	1:21	1:47, 69; 2:11
Jesus comes from the Davidic line	1:1, 16-17, 20	1:27, 32, 69
Jesus is born in Bethlehem	2:1	2:4, 11
Jesus is born under the time of Herod the Great	2:1	1:5
Mary, Joseph, and Jesus live in Nazareth	2:22-23	2:39, 51

APPENDIX B: ADVENT

Advent is primetime real estate for churches. This is when families start piling into churches and watch people light candles while they quietly rest their eyes and wait for the minister to say Amen so they can make their way with the family to the promised buffet brunch.

I bet if you asked most people what Advent is, they'd say with confidence, "Oh, it's that thing we do before Christmas!"

And if you follow up with, "Yeah, but why?" they'd probably shrug their shoulders and look at you confused; perhaps they'd give you a stink eye because you're going to be that wise guy who tries to spoil their brunch buffet.

If you are reading a book on Christmas, then it's obviously important for you to be that person at Christmas who ruins the buffet brunch by being the one to say, "What is Advent?" So strap in for a short, bumpy ride.

The elevator pitch for Advent is, "prepare us for Christmas."

Advent is to Christmas as Lent is to Easter. Orthodox Christians even time box it at 40 days like Lent—though others do not.

The history of Advent, however, is murky at best. So even if you ask your minister why we celebrate, they're going to have some difficulty explaining it.

THE MURKY HISTORY OF ADVENT SEASON

If you are thinking, "well, heck! What's the point of celebrating if we don't even know why?" you aren't without reason. But like most traditions, there are foundations for Advent. We don't celebrate them because we know with certainty that this is some Biblical date—half the time their origins are not even Biblical. We celebrate them for what they represent.

In the case of Advent, it represents the time that we prepare ourselves for Christmas.

So let's stop and think about that for a minute: Prepare yourself for Christmas.

When you think of it like that, it makes you think about it differently.

It is not to prepare in the sense that you need to get all those presents so you can tell all your friends you are that person who is all done shopping with two months left to go. Or prepare in the sense that you are going to make that really thoughtful gift.[95]

What does prepare yourself mean then? It means Christmas represents the day that God gave you the ultimate gift. Prepare yourself spiritually to receive it. Reflect on what it

[95] Crochet new underwear, for that person in your life who loves to walk around itchy.

means for you—and what it means for how you are supposed to treat others.

Advent is most definitely a time to come around with family and celebrate, but that's only part of the story.

As best as anyone can tell, Advent first began to be celebrated around 500 AD, give or take. The Council of Tours in 567,[96] which said monks and priest couldn't marry, also said there was to be an Advent period before Christmas.

So what we know is in 567, a bunch of monks and priest got together expecting their annual Christmas bonus, and instead were told on top of no bonus, they'd also have to forget about ever marrying, and they needed to take a few weeks to reflect on what it meant to never have sex again. Up until this time, they actually could marry—and many, in fact, had married. So next time you think your Christmas was bad, think about the Council of 567, which gave perhaps the most killjoy gifts ever.

Advent is one of the simpler holidays in Christianity. It's not rooted in complex, and sometimes weird, theology. It's as simple as preparing your heart for Christmas. That's it. So before making a beeline for the ribs, give it some time to reflect on that. Don't think about how good you got it. Reflect—pray—about where you would be if that Christmas gift named Jesus never showed up under your Christmas tree. Who would you be? Spend 40 days making this devotion part of your day before Christmas and see how it makes you feel

---

[96] Not to be confused with the Council of Tour de France, in which all the bishops got together to show off their extreme biking skills while discussing theology.

when Christmas comes. You might just think of it like you never have before.

APPENDIX C: THE CONDENSED HISTORY OF CHRISTMAS PAST

The Nativity story isn't quite what we heard in Sunday school, but what about Christmas? Have we really been celebrating Christmas with mistletoes hanging under the doorway, Christmas trees in front of the fireplace, and carolers at our front doors since the birth of Christ?

Not quite.

Christmas has a checkered and colorful past. Contrary to what we may want to believe, Christmas didn't start the day Jesus was born. And it didn't start right after he died because we wanted a day to remember him. It actually came hundreds of years later—sort of. And it evolved over time.

You probably have your own ideas of it—that it came from some pagan holiday and Christians used it somehow to convert these pagans; that Santa was some gift-giving saint. There's definitely some truth to all of this, but even here, there are elements of fiction. So let's look at the real(ly condensed) history of Christmas.

THE GIFT OF GIFT-GIVING

The real main event around Christmas is gift-giving.

It sort of makes sense to say we give gifts because the Magi gave gifts. Sort of. But how did we arrive there? How did we get from giving gifts to Christ to giving gifts to each other? How did we get from the manger to storming Target on Christmas Eve, grabbing whatever is left, and wrapping it with seconds to spare? Like most Christmas traditions, it evolved over time.

Romans had a custom of giving gifts around New Years, and Christians just bumped it up a few days and said it represented the gifts brought to Jesus by the Wise Men.

But it's not quite that simple. Gift-giving had a relatively bumpy road; the gift-giving we know today is largely linked to New York at the turn of the century. Christmas was a time of celebration and drunkenness—public displays of misgivings were pretty common in the streets of New York during the mid-1800s. It was one giant street party. Some New Yorkers began to worry about things getting a little too rowdy, so they started to promote the idea of bringing Christmas celebrations into their home and making it more family-oriented.

Flagship stores like Macy's began getting decked out with toys around this time.[97] Christmas got a little more personal, but it also got a little more commercial.

---

[97] Fun fact: Iceland has a tradition called Jolabokaflod (i.e. the Christmas book flood); families exchange books and then read

WHERE DID SANTA REALLY COME FROM?

The greatest Christmas folklore of them all is that of Jolly Saint Nick (AKA Santa Claus). I'm sure you've heard a few stories of his invention. The only Santa canon I hold to be true is found in the movie *The Santa Claus 1* and *2*.[98]

The so-called "historic Santa" goes way back to Turkey—around 280 AD.

This is what we know about good old St. Nicky: There was a real man named Nicholas of Bari. He lived in Turkey.

That's it.

The problem with tracing the historical Santa is pretty much all the text we have about him come from a text written long after he was dead. The text, hence, can be seen as more folklore than history.

We can probably assume that he came from a wealthy family, and he used his inherited wealth to help the less fortunate. Some say he gave up his wealth and became a monk. Maybe that's true. Maybe it's not.

He is believed to have been the Bishop of Myra, and some think he was at the Council of Nicaea. The one that basically cemented the idea of the trinity.

But this is only one tradition. The problem with Santa is the Dutch, the Swedish, and pretty much every European nation had its own folklore that felt a bit Santa-like. Germans,

---

them in the evening. It's on December 24, and this book would make an excellent choice for those Icelanders in your life.

[98] Let's just pretend The Santa Claus 3 never existed, shall we? Martin Short, I love you, but Jack Frost, you are not.

for example, celebrated an event called Yule where a long-bearded figure would appear on a horse. He would enter houses through fire holes (or chimneys). He was pagan at first because this was prior to Christianity, but the figure slowly began to take on the traditions of Santa that were sweeping the world.

But how do we get from creepy, weird folklore Santa to Jolly Saint Nick stuffing his oversized figure down a chimney? Many point to the 1823 poem *A Visit from St. Nicholas*.[99] There's certainly truth there. Many of the traditions we know today are found in that poem. But it was really the entire 19th century we can thank; throughout the century, Santa is popping up in articles, cartoons, and books everywhere. Dicken's *A Christmas Carol* may be one of the best-known Christmas tales, but even L. Frank Baum took a crack at him with his 1902 publication, *The Life and Adventures of Santa Claus*.

Santa arrived at department stores in 1890 thanks to an entrepreneur and child at heart, James Edgar. Edgar, looking to drum up business for his department store in Brockton, Massachusetts (about an hour south of Boston, Massachusetts), started dressing up as Santa to the delight of children. At first, he kept it in his store, but would later walk up and down the street. People from as far away as Rhode Island would come to meet him. While it was definitely good for business, Edgar made sure to stay true to Santa's legacy of giving back; he was known for paying the medical expenses of children in hospitals and giving young adults their first jobs.

---

[99] Known more popularly as 'Twas the Night Before Christmas.'

Photography was still a bit expensive when Edgar paraded down the streets greeting children, so people didn't come to take a photo with him. The tradition of taking your photo with Santa didn't start for nearly 30 years. By 1918, we start seeing photos of kids with Santa popping up all over the place.

CHRISTMAS IS CANCELED

Amongst Christmas' somewhat messy past is the most epic bah humbug of them all: when Christians kind of sort of canceled Christmas.

For hundreds of years, Christmas had evolved into a less than Christian event where you partied a little too hard. The Protestant reformation got into full swing and began suggesting we ban it, citing it was basically just an excuse to get drunk and sin. Puritans took it up a notch and pointed out that its root in solstice history made it a little demonic and took away the message of Christ.

This was going on across Europe, but it was really England who was hit the hardest. By 1647, Charles I issued a decree to officially ban the holiday.

After the decree in England, Christmas became sort of the original prohibition. Yes, it was banned, but that just made celebrating it more daring. People began celebrating it in secret.[100]

It didn't take long for a hero to come along to redeem the repressed holiday, and in Christmas' case, that hero was

[100] Imagine little Timmy walking into mom and dad's bedroom and discovering the secret Christmas stash under the bed—he'd need therapy for life!

Charles II. He was looking for a way to show his commoners just how much of a bad boy he was, and Christmas became his symbolic gesture. By 1681, Christmas was officially legal again. Legalized didn't mean pastors were puffing the jolly pipes from the pulpit; many ministers, notably led by Cotton Mather,[101] condemned the holiday and preached that it was essentially for secular fools. Mather was basically the original Scrooge—the man who could take the happiest time of year—and turn it into a lecture of how terrible we all are. It was like your friend inviting you to their birthday party, which would have a bounce house; and then you get there, and you discover that it's no birthday party at all—it's a meeting to tell you all about Amway. And there will be no bounce house.

And if you are sitting there thinking: so people calling Christmas a secular holiday isn't anything new? Then consider this: you can kind of blame Puritans' condemnation of Christmas for the rise of secular forms of the holiday. While they were sitting in church huffing and puffing about how secular the holiday was, non-Puritans were only adding to it—replacing Christian aspects with more secular aspects. So if you are angry that Christmas isn't Christian enough, you can thank Christians for making it less Christian.

CHRISTMAS IS REBORN

The death of Christmas was largely tied to England. Elsewhere around the world, things weren't quite as dire. In

[101] The puritanical nut who started the Salem Witch Trials.

Germany, for example, Christmas had very much been in full swing.

So when Queen Victoria decided to get all lovey-dovey with her German cousin Prince Albert,[102] he brought with him a bunch of Christmas baggage.

Once the kissing cousins began popping them out, Prince Albert wanted to share his German Christmas traditions with his children. Royal watchers[103] took notice and wanted a Christmas of their own.

Things really started sizzling for Christmas in 1848 when the cover of the Illustrated London News featured a tantalizing picture of the royal family around a Christmas tree. Christmas trees were not exactly anything new for Germans[104], but this brilliant display of nature in the living room started a craze in England—anyone who was anyone wanted a tree of their very own. Today, it's estimated that over 30 million trees are sold in the United States alone—all thanks to an incestuous royal couple.

While the royals and their watchers were eating Christmas up, the holiday was still a little meh across the pond in America. It wasn't declared a federal holiday until 1870—nearly 100 years after the country was formed. You can thank those department stores for that.

---

[102] Not the distant third cousin twice removed sort of cousin—they were firsties all the way.

[103] Who were basically the upper-class.

[104] The history of Christmas trees is also pretty murky; one popular legend links it to Martin Luther—who tradition says was walking in the forest one day and was blown away by a magnificent tree, so he cut it down and brought it home to his family.

FURTHER READING

No book is born on its own. Rather it's born from the ideas and inspiration of books that came before it.

During the writing of this book, I researched several books on both the history and theology behind Christmas.

While I do not support the theology behind all of these books, I nonetheless recommend them for readers who want to further explore the magic, mystery and love of Christmas.

Christmas: A Short History From Solstice to Santa - Andy Thomas - Ivy Press, London, England - 2019

Mystery of the Magi: The Quest to Identify the Three Wise Men - Dwight Longenecker - Regnery History, Washington DC - 2019

The First Christmas: What the Gospels Really Teach About Jesus's Birth - Marcus J. Borg & John Dominic Crossan - Harper One, New York NY - 2007

C Is For Christmas: The History, Personalities, and Meaning of Christ's Birth - David W. Wiersbe and Warren W. Wiersbe - Baker Books, Grand Rapid, Michigan - 2012

The Characters of Christmas: The Unlikely People Caught Up in the Story of Jesus - Daniel Darling - Moody Publishers, Chicago IL - 2019

Hidden Christmas: The Surprising Truth Behind the Birth of Christ - Timothy Keller - Penguin Books, New York NY - 2016

Bethlehem: Biography of a Town - Nicholas Blincoe - Nation Books, New York, NY – 2017

ORGANIC FAITH SERIES

These books are part of the *Organic Faith* series. The series takes Biblical topics, and strips them down to their purist state so you can reconsider them in ways you may have never thought about before.

Learn more about the series and future books at www.JesusAscended.com.

MORE TO COME

Many years ago, I wrote humor for the now defunct Christian humor magazine the *Wittenburg Door*. If you'd like to read the parodies I wrote there, join my newsletter list and I'll send you out a free copy.

Join here: https://www.jesusascended.com/newsletter

In addition to a free book, I'll occasionally (interpret as hardly ever) email you about new books and other writing news you might enjoy.

ABOUT THE AUTHOR

Scott Douglas wrote this about page, which, he admits, makes him sound a bit like a narcissist; so narcissistically speaking, Douglas is the esteemed author of a memoir about his experience working in a public library (*Quiet, Please: Dispatches from a Public Librarian)*, an ongoing YA series (*The N00b Warriors)*, and two technical books on iPhone app development (*Going Mobile* and *Build Your Own Apps for Fun and Profit*). Esteemed writing aside, Douglas teaches humor and memoir writing for the Gotham Writers Workshops. He lives in Anaheim, but to sound cooler, he usually says he "lives five minutes from Disneyland." He lives with his wife, Diana, in a home that is a registered California landmark.

If you enjoyed this book, you may also enjoy his apologetics work *#OrganicJesus: Finding Your Way to An Unprocessed, GMO-Free Christianity* (Kregel 2016)

If Scott Douglas did not write this about page, it would read: Scott Douglas lives in Anaheim with his wife. He is the author of other books. He likes to think that his organic deodorant holds back his BO for more than 30 minutes, but who is he kidding?

You can connect with him and find out about his newest books here: www.ScottDouglas.org/mailinglist

Lightning Source UK Ltd.
Milton Keynes UK
UKHW010729010822
406672UK00002B/407

9 781629 175270